arcola
theatre

An Enemy
of the People

by Henrik Ibsen

a new version by Rebecca Lenkiewicz

from a literal translation by Charlotte Barslund

First performed at Arcola Theatre on 1 April 2008

An Enemy of the People

The action takes place in a coastal town in Southern Norway in the late nineteenth century

Cast

Greg Hicks	**DR THOMAS STOCKMANN** Medical Officer at the Baths
Alison McKenna	**CATHERINE STOCKMANN** His wife
Fiona O'Shaughnessy	**PETRA** Their daughter, a schoolteacher
Christopher Godwin	**PETER STOCKMANN** Thomas' brother, Mayor
Robin Browne	**MORTEN KIIL** Master tanner, Mrs Stockmann's foster father
Daniel Rabin	**HOVSTAD** Editor of *The People's Messenger*
Chris Moran	**BILLING** An employee at the *Messenger*
Jim Bywater	**ASLASKEN** A printer
Sean Campion	**HORSTER** A sea captain

Production Team

Director	Mehmet Ergen
Set Design	Jason Southgate
Costume Design	Lorna Ritchie
Lighting Design	Michael Nabarro
Sound Design	Adrienne Quartly
Assistant Director	Fiona Morrell
Production Manager	Martin Barron
Production Assistant	Onur Cihan
Stage Manager	David Salter
Press	Anne Mayer
Photography	Simon Annand

arcola
theatre

Arcola Theatre was founded in September 2000 when Mehmet Ergen and Leyla Nazlı converted a textile factory on the borders of Stoke Newington/ Dalston into one of London's largest and most adaptable Off-West End venues. Arcola is now one of the country's most renowned theatres with a distinct and powerful identity both within in the local community and British theatre.

Since its foundation Arcola Theatre has won the Peter Brook Empty Space Award two years in a row and was given the Time Out Live Award twice for 'Inventive Programming on a Shoestring' in 2003 and 'Favourite Fringe Venue' in 2005/6. A large number of its productions have been selected as Critic's Choice in Time Out and the national newspapers. It has gained a reputation for staging work by some of the best actors, writers and directors including productions by William Gaskill, Dominic Droomgoole, Max Stafford-Clark, David Farr, Bonnie Greer, Adam Rapp, Sam Shepherd, Eric Schossler, Helena Kaut-Howson and Kathryn Hunter.

In 2003 Arcola was said to '*live on love and hope rather than money*' (The Independent). This year, with a staff of just eleven, and a 40 percent increase in our Arts Council grant, '*Arcola looks like a mean, lean machine revving up for new challenges*' (Michael Coveney, What's On Stage).

Arcola's open door ethos continues to keep belts tights and life vibrant in a spirit of constant innovation. Our Arcola Energy project is pushing back the eco-cultural frontier, pioneering LED lighting technology and sustainable production processes with the help of key partnerships including Mayor of London, Arts Council, London Hydrogen Partnership, Hackney Council, DCMS, Pixel Range, London Calling, Whitelight, ETC and Central School of Speech and Drama.

For Arcola Theatre

Mehmet Ergen	Artistic Director
Ben Todd	Executive Director
Leyla Nazlı	Executive Producer
Michael John Harris	General Manager
Nicole Rosner	Finance Manager
Lilli Geissendorfer	Commercial Manager
David Salter	Technical Manager
Gemma Greer	Front of House Manager
Lauretta Barrow	Front of House Manager
Jasmine Rowe	Front of House Manager

Cast Biographies

Robin Browne (*Morten Kiil*)

Robin began his career in Liverpool and made his West End debut, in 1969, in Eric Porter's production of *My Little Boy My Big Girl.* He went on to play Rusty in the original series of *Crossroads.* As a member of the Peter Hall company he played opposite Julie Walters and Ken Stott in *The Rose Tattoo* and was Phipps in *An Ideal Husband.* Other theatre credits include *House And Garden* (NT), *Murder At The Vicarage, The Constant Wife* (West End), *As You Like It* (Peter Hall USA tour), *Allegiance* (Assembly Rooms, Edinburgh), *Swing* (BAC).

U.K. television credits include *Z Cars, Crossroads, It Ain't Half Hot Mum, Macbeth, Cause Celebre, Outside Edge, Hammer House of Horror, Public Eye, Wycliffe, Grange Hill, The Upper Hand,* Peter Hall's TV film *The Final Passage, The Hunter And The Hunted, Judge John Deed, Panorama: The Hutton Inquiry,* and most recently *Little Britain.*

Robin was also associate producer of the world premiere of the Vivienne Ellis award winning musical *Bon Voyage.* He co-founded The Harry Partnership LLP, a communications skills company, 20 years ago.

Jim Bywater (*Aslasken*)

Recent theatre credits include *Chasing the Moment* (Arcola, NT Studio, Southwark Playhouse, Edinburgh Festival, Israel), *Merchant of Venice* (Globe), *Blitz, Importance of Being Earnest, The Ghost Train, Sleeping Beauty, Jack and the Beanstalk, Mother Goose* (all Queen's Theatre, Essex), *Measure for Measure, King Lear, Two Gentlemen of Verona* (all Globe).

Jim has worked for the Tie department, producing material which deals with immigration, bullying and literature (*To Kill a Mockingbird, MacBeth* (director), *Animal Farm* – adapter and director), healthy lifestyles (*Olivia Twist* – writer and director) and *Missing Dan Nolan* (director).

Sean Campion (*Horster*)

Sean has held many leading roles, including most recently *Othello* (Sailsbury Playhouse), *Carthage Must Be Destroyed* (Traverse Theatre), *Food* (Traverse Theatre, Fringe First), *Phaedra* and *The Cosmonaut's Last Message To The Woman He Once Loved In The Former Soviet Union* (both Donmar Warehouse), *Blackwater Angel* (Finborough Theatre), *The Quare Fellow* (Oxford Stage Company, UK tour & Tricycle Theatre), and Jake Quinn in *Stones in His Pockets* (West End, Broadway and other venues) for which is he was nominated for the Lawrence Olivier Award and Tony Award.

TV credits include *Holby City* (BBC), *Eastenders* (BBC), *Blackwater Lightship* (Hallmark Hall of Fame/World 2000), *Timbuktu* (Yellow Asylum Films), *Goldfish Memory* (Goldfish Films).

Christopher Godwin (*Peter Stockmann*)

Christopher's numerous theatre credits include *Canterbury Tales, The Taming of the Shrew, The Tamer Tamed, Cymbeline, The Devil is an Ass, The Relapse, Woyzeck* (all RSC), *Love's Labours Lost, We the People* (Globe), *Professor Bernhardi, Musik* (Arcola), *Home* (OSC), *Henry 1V Part 1, Romeo and Juliet, As You Like It, Love's Labours Lost, Twelfth Night, Troilus and Cressida* (Regent's Park), *The Woman in Black, What a Performance, Noises Off, Ten Times Table, Hay Fever, School for Scandal* (West End), *The Guv'nor* (Young Vic).

Television credits include *Waking the Dead, Innocents, Nice Work, My Family and Other Animals.*

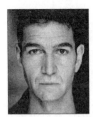

Greg Hicks (*Dr Thomas Stockmann*)

Greg's extensive theatre credits include numerous plays for the National Theatre as well as long spells at the RSC and The Old Vic. He won the 2006 TMA Award for Best Perfomance in a Play for *Tamburlaine the Great* (Bristol/Old Vic/Barbican). Recent theatre credits include the title role in *Don Quixote* (West Yorkshire Playhouse), *Angels in America* (Headlong/Lyric Hammersmith), *The Lady of Leisure* (Liverpool Playhouse), *Missing Persons* (Trafalgar Studios and Assembly Rooms, Edinburgh Festival Nomination Best Performance), *Macbeth* and *Hamlet* (RSC), *Messiah* (Old Vic), *Coriolanus* (Critics Circle Award, Olivier Nomination), *Merry Wives Of Windsor* (Old Vic and RSC), *Bacchae* (NT), *Julius Caesar, Tantalus, Family Reunion* (RSC), *Salome* (Riverside Studio), *The Relapse, Enrico IV, Private Lives, Venice Preserved, 1953* (Citizens Theatre), *King Lear, Waiting For Godot, The Seagull, Waste* (Old Vic), *The Oedipus Plays* and *Absolute Hell* (NT), *Piaf* (Piccadilly), *Total Eclipse* (Greenwich), *Murder By Misadventure* (Vaudeville), *The Homecoming* (Comedy Theatre), *The Day You'll Love Me* (Hampstead), *Vanilla* (Lyric), *Les Liaisons Dangereuses* (Ambassadors), *Romeo And Juliet* (RSC).

Television credits include *Trail & Retribution* (La Plante Productions), *Waking The Dead* (BBC), *Tiberius Gracchus, Aemilianus* (BBC), *The Ten Commandments* (Hallmark), *Guardian* (ITV).

Alison McKenna (*Mrs Catherine Stockmann*)

Alison trained at the Samuel Beckett Centre, Trinity College, Dublin.

Irish theatre credits include *Tic* (Talltales Theatre Co.), *Hysteria* (Project Arts Centre Theatre, nominated for Best Actress, Irish Times Awards 2007), *The Cherry Orchard, The Importance of Being Earnest, The Colleen Bawn* (nominated for Irish Times ESB Best Supporting Actress Award), *She Stoops to Folly, Six Characters in Search of an Author* (all for Abbey Theatre), *Jane Eyre, Pride and Prejudice, Great Expectations, Aristocrats* (all Gate Theatre, Dublin and in *Aristocrats*, NY).

In the UK theatre credits include *The Gigli Concert* (Assembly Rooms, Edinburgh), *Mutabilitie, Night of the Iguana* (both NT), *A Woman of No Importance, The*

Colleen Bawn (both Manchester Royal Exchange), *The Hostage* (RSC, Barbican), *The Glass Menagerie* (Watford Palace) and *Hysteria* (Minerva Theatre, Chichester).

Film and Television appearances include *The Clinic* (Parallell Films), *The Bill* (ITV), *The Cassidys* (RTE), *Pie in the Sky* (Select TV), *The Ambassador* (Ecosse Films), *Bossanova Blues* (RCA), *The Actors* (Company of Wolves Productions) and *The American* (BBC Films).

Alison is co-founder of b*spoke theatre company.

Chris Moran (*Billing*)

Chris trained at Lamda. He won the Carleton Hobbs award and was a member of the BBC Radio Drama Company for six months. His theatre credits include *Dead Hands* (The Wrestling School), *Animaux en Paradis* (Theatre Deux Rives, Rouen), *My Boy Jack* (National Tour), *Donkeys' Years* (Comedy Theatre) and *Making History* (Ouroboros). Most recently he appeared in *The Six-Days World* (Finborough) and in a one man show, *Treading the Boards* (Rosemary Branch Theatre).

Fiona O'Shaughnessy (*Petra*)

Fiona's theatre credits include the title role of *Salome* (Gate Theatre, Dublin). Also for the Gate Theatre *See You Next Tuesday, Blythe Spirit, Oliver, The Importance of Being Earnest, Pride and Prejudice, Arms and the Man*. For the Abbey, Dublin/West End *The Shaughraun*. Other theatre credits include *Honour* (B*Spoke), *Blackwater Angel* (Finborough), *Country* (Archlight), *Fando and Us* (Siren) and *Blasted* (Bedrock).

Film and TV credits include, most recently, *The Stronger* (Lia Williams for Tightrope). Also, *Nightwatching* with Peter Greenaway, *Trouble in Paradise* (RTE), *Malice Aforethought* (Mountview Films), *Meeting Che Guevara and the Man from Maybury Hill, Villains, Mea Culpa* (igloo), *Goldfish Memory* (Liz Gill, Goldfish Films), *Halo Effect* (Lance Daly, Fastnet) and *Alexander* (Oliver Stone, Warner Brothers).

Daniel Rabin (*Hovstad*)

Daniel trained at Central School of Speech and Drama. Recent theatre credits include *All Quiet On The Western Front* (Nottingham Playhouse), *Shoreditch Madonna* (Soho Theatre), *Chicken Soup with Barley* (Tricycle/Nottingham Playhouse), *Achidi J's Final Hours* (Finborough), *Coffee Lovers Guide to America* (Chelsea Theatre), Corpus Christi (Pleasance), *The Last Sortie* (New End), *The Seven Sonnets of Michaelangelo* (Lyric Hammersmith).

TV credits include *Eastenders* (BBC), *Casualty* (BBC), *Spooks* (BBC), *The Roman Mysteries* (BBC), *Money Can't Buy You Love* (C4), *Family Affairs* (C5). Film credits include *Mind the Gap, Penalty King, Bury It, Fly Fishing, Down, Away* and *Susie Gold*.

Production Team Biographies

Martin Barron (Production Manager)

Martin trained at Guildhall School of Music & Drama and has a filmmaking diploma from the New York Film Academy. Theatre credits include *Big White Fog, Enemies, The Late Henry Moss* and *Brighton Rock* (all Almeida Theatre). He has also worked extensively with the Almeida Theatre's Projects department. Prior to his work at the Almeida, Martin performed, directed and ran drama workshops at the Santa Monica Playhouse in California. Martin is a co-founder of Blue Scream Theatre; credits include *The Adventures of Tom Thumb* (Edinburgh Festival, Fringe First Award), *The Day of Nine Dogs* (CPT) and *The Invisibles* (BAC).

Production management work includes *La Boheme, Cosi Fan Tutte, Cenerentola* and *Don Giovanni* for the Garden Opera Company. Martin was Technical Stage Manager for The Opera Group's *The Shops*.

Charlotte Barslund (Translator)

Charlotte translates Scandinavian plays and novels. Her translation of Strindberg's *The Pelican* with Janet McTeer was broadcast on BBC Radio 3. She translated Ingmar Bergman's version of *Ghosts* by Henrik Ibsen, which was performed at the Barbican Theatre. Her translation of the Norwegian crime novel *Calling Out For You!* by Karin Fossum was nominated for the 2005 Gold Dagger Award by the British Crime Writers' Association. Other translated novels include *Machine* by Peter Adolphsen and *Black Seconds* by Karin Fossum.

Onur Cihan (Production Assistant)

Onur has a BA in Radio, Television and Film from Ankara University and is doing a Masters in Children's Theatre and Educational Drama. He has directed and produced some short films and documentaries which have been awarded at several film festivals. His acting credits include *The Game is Up* by J-P. Sartre, *The Little Match Girl* by H.C. Andersen, *The Shadow of the Donkey* by H. Taner, *Killing the Rat* by I. Yalcin, *Looking at the Stars* by B. Necatigil.

Mehmet Ergen (Director)

Mehmet is Founder and Artistic Director of the Arcola Theatre; co-founder and the first artistic director of the Southwark Playhouse (1993-1999). Directing work for the Arcola: *Silver Birch House* by Leyla Nazli, *Chasing the Moment* by Jack Shepherd, *The Plebeians Rehearse the Uprising* by Günter Grass, *Jitterbug* by Bonnie Greer, *A Midsummer Night's Dream* and *Macbeth* by W. Shakespeare (both with Jack Shepherd).

Other theatre work includes *Afterplay* by Brian Friel, *Noises Off* by Michael Frayn, *Lieutenant of Inishmore* by Martin McDonagh, *The Betrayal, Ashes to Ashes, One for the Road* by Harold Pinter, *The Shape of Things* by Neil LaBute, *Fool for Love* by Sam Shepard, *The Nest* by Kroetz, *Much Ado About Nothing* and *King Lear* by William Shakespeare, *Roots* by Arnold Wesker, *Of Mice and Men* by John Steinbeck, *The Protagonist* by Georg Kaiser, *In the Jungle of the Cities, Informer, Exception and the Rule* by Bertold Brecht, *Mandragola* by Machiavelli. Operas and musicals include *Seven Deadly Sins* by Brecht / Weill, *I Can Get It For You Wholesale* by J Weidman / Harold Rome (both for Arcola Theatre), *Dorian* (Arts Theatre, West

End), *Treemonisha* by Scott Joplin, *Lost in the Stars* by Kurt Weill, *The Cradle Will Rock* by Marc Blitzstein (all at BAC).

His translations include works by Henric Ibsen, Harold Pinter, Sam Shepard, Neil LaBute and Martin McDonagh. Mehmet is currently opening Arcola Istanbul.

Rebecca Lenkiewicz (Writer)

Rebecca's stage plays include *Soho – A Tale of Table Dancers* (Edinburgh Festival Fringe First, Israel tour with British Council, opening of Arcola Theatre 2001), *The Night Season* (National Theatre, Cottesloe, nominated for an Evening Standard Award, the Susan Smith Blackburn Award and won the Critics' Circle Award 2004 for Most Promising Playwright), *Shoreditch Madonna* (Soho Theatre, 2005), adaptation of Stravinsky's *The Soldier's Tale* (Old Vic), *Blue Moon Over Poplar* (NYT/Soho Theatre), *Invisible Mountains* (NT Education Department), *Justitia* (for the Jasmin Vardimon Dance Company, UK Tour and Sadlers Wells). Radio plays include *Fighting for Words* (BBC, Observer Critics' Choice, Pick of the Day), *Caravan Of Desire* (BBC, Telegraph Critics' Choice, Radio Times Choice, Pick of the Week), *Blue Moon Over Poplar* (BBC). Rebecca has adapted *The Sea Change* by Elizabeth Jane Howard into a screenplay for Fragile Films. She is presently under commission to the Royal National Theatre who will produce her next play *Her Naked Skin* on the Olivier stage in July 2008.

Fiona Morrell (Assistant Director)

Fiona's directing credits include *The Alice Project* at BAC and CPT, *National Amnesty & Acquaintances* by Dom Mitchell at The Pleasance, Islington, *A Life Less Ordinary People* by Peter Yates at Theatre 503 and *Cabaret* by Kander & Ebb at The Bloomsbury Theatre. She has also directed readings at The Old Vic, The Hampstead Theatre and the Arcola.

As assistant director she has worked on *The Water's Edge* by Theresa Rebeck at Second Stage Theatre, New York and *The Hypochondriac* by Molière at the Almeida Theatre. She has also worked on a variety of theatre education projects. Fiona was runner-up for the 2007 JMK Directors' Award and awarded a Winston Churchill Fellowship to study theatre in New York.

Michael Nabarro (Lighting Design)

Michael is a graduate of the RADA Lighting Design course.

Lighting credits include *The Blind* (Arcola Theatre), *Limbo* & *1984* (York Theatre Royal), *Rivers Run Deep* & *Fight Fight Fight!* (Hampstead Theatre Studio), *Gabriel, In the Heart of America, Salome, Duck Hunting* & *The Girl on the Sofa* (Royal Academy of Dramatic Art), *The Ash Girl* (Unicorn Theatre), *White People* & *Cocoa* (Theatre 503), *Singin' in the Rain, West Side Story* & *Orpheus in the Underworld* (Cambridge Arts Theatre), *Of Two Days* (Pleasance, London), *The Revenger's Tragedy* & CASA Latin American Theatre Festival (St Andrew's Crypt).

Michael graduated from Cambridge University in 2003 and between 2003 and 2006 was manager of the ADC Theatre in Cambridge.

Adrienne Quartly (Sound Design)

Theatre credits include include *Nostalgia* (Drum Plymouth), *The Stage Coach* (Derry), *Stockholm* (Frantic Assembly), *The Container* (Edinburgh 07), *Woyzeck* (NYC), *93.2FM* (Royal Court), *Hysteria,* (Mime festival), *Silver Birch House* (Arcola), *Hideaway* (Complicite), *Amedee,* Young Vic, *My Real War* (National Tour), *Playing For Time, A Touch Of The Sun* (Salisbury Playhouse), *Last Waltz Season* (Arcola), *Mercy Fine* (Clean Break), *Tejas Verdes* (Gate) *Attempts On Her Life* (BAC), *Jarman Garden, NAO* (as a cellist), *Inflated Ideas* (Riverside), *Habeas Corpus* (Royal Theatre, Northampton).

Lorna Ritchie (Costume Design)

Set and costume design credits include *Mules* (Young Vic), *The Car Cemetery* (The Gate), *Limbo* (York Theatre Royal and touring), *Wuthering Heights* (York Theatre Royal). Lorna was awarded the Linbury Biennale Prize for Stage Design Finalist 2007 and the Royal Shakespeare Company Design Scholarship 2006-2007.

David Salter (Stage Manager)

David is Technical Manager and resident Stage Manager at the Arcola Theatre. He has worked on both incoming and in-house productions, including *Purgatorio, Factory Girls, Mariana Pineda, Great Theatre of the World,* and the *National Theatre Connections Festival.* Other productions include *My Arm* (BAC and Tate Modern), *Danny's Wake* (Sound, Leicester Square), *Lear* (Glasgow Repertory Company), *Baron Munchausen* (Southwark Playhouse) and *Julius Caesar* (Young Vic). He has also worked on site-specific performances, toured shows with Quantum Theatre, and worked with *Hart Ryan TV Productions, 20-20 Television, Blast Theory,* and at the Royal Albert Hall.

Jason Southgate (Set Design)

Jason was born in Liverpool and trained at Central St Martins, he received an Arts Council Design Bursary in 2000. Recently he has designed *Waiting for Godot, Peter Pan, Desire Under the Elms, Hamlet, The Bevellers* and *James and the Giant Peach* (all for the Citizens Theatre Glasgow). Recent Opera designs include *Der Silbersee, Wexford Festival, Turn of the Screw, Landestheater Salzburg, Tannhauser, Stadtheatre Minden, La Cenerentola* (Frankfurt Opera) and *Armide* (Buxton Festival).

29 April – 31 May
8 pm and Sat 3.30 pm (excl. 3rd)

Arcola Theatre and Silkensaw present

The Lady from the Sea

by **Henrik Ibsen**

a new version by **Frank McGuinness**

directed by **Hannah Eidinow**

Lia Williams stars in a sensuous and erotic play about the power of the past. Ellida's desires are awakened by the startling arrival of a dark stranger, luring her back to the water's edge . . .

Book Now on 0207 503 1646
or online arcolatheatre.com

Henrik Ibsen
An Enemy of the People

a new version by
REBECCA LENKIEWICZ

from a literal translation by
Charlotte Barslund

faber and faber

First published in 2008
by Faber and Faber Limited
3 Queen Square London WC1N 3AU

Typeset by Country Setting, Kingsdown, Kent CT14 8ES
Printed in England by CPI Bookmarque Ltd, Croydon, Surrey

A CIP record for this book
is available from the British Library

ISBN 978-0-571-24259-7

2 4 6 8 10 9 7 5 3 1

Rebecca Lenkiewicz would like to thank
Mel Kenyon, Leyla Nazli, Dinah Wood,
Mehmet Ergen, Ben Todd, Michael Harris
and everyone at the Arcola Theatre

Characters

Dr Thomas Stockmann
Medical Officer at the Baths

Catherine Stockmann
his wife

Petra
their daughter, a schoolteacher

Peter Stockmann
Thomas's brother, Mayor, Chief Constable,
and Chairman of the Baths Committee

Morten Kiil
Master Tanner, Mrs Stockmann's foster father

Hovstad
editor of *The People's Messenger*

Billing
an employee at *The People's Messenger*

Horster
a sea captain

Aslaksen
a printer

Townspeople
present at a public meeting

*The action takes place in a coastal town
in Southern Norway*

AN ENEMY OF THE PEOPLE

Act One

*Dr Stockmann's living room. Evening. The décor is
modest but neat. There are two doors on the right-hand
wall, the furthest leading to the hall and the nearest to
Stockmann's study. On the left-hand wall is a far door
that leads to the family's other rooms. A tiled stove
stands against this wall. There is a sofa, and next to it
an oval table with a cloth on it and a lighted lamp with
a shade. Above the sofa is a mirror. At the back of the
room an open door leads to the dining room, where the
table has been set. There is a lamp on the dinner table.*

*Billing sits at the table, a napkin tucked into his shirt.
Mrs Stockmann stands beside him, holding a plate with
a large joint of beef. There is nobody else at the table,
but there are remnants of food and drink from those
who have just eaten.*

Billing This is wonderful.

Mrs Stockmann It can't be, it's cold.

Billing No, it's absolutely fantastic, Mrs Stockmann.

Mrs Stockmann My husband. He's very fixed about
what time he eats.

Billing I'm so sorry I was late. But really this suits me
down to the ground, I promise you. It's all the joy of
eating and the added bliss of not having to talk to anyone.

Mrs Stockmann As long as you're happy.

A noise from the hall.

That must be Mr Hovstad.

Billing (*shouting through to the hall*) You took your time, Hov!

Mayor Peter Stockmann enters, wearing an overcoat and his official hat. He carries a stick.

Mayor Good evening, Catherine.

Mrs Stockmann enters the living room.

Mrs Stockmann Oh. Peter. Good evening. We weren't . . . this is a pleasant surprise.

Mayor I was in the area. (*He glances towards the dining room.*) Ah. I see it's not a good time.

Mrs Stockmann (*a touch embarrassed*) Oh no no, not at all. Come. Sit down. Have you eaten?

Mayor A cooked meal after six? No.

Mrs Stockmann Just the once would do no harm, would it?

Mayor I've had my tea and sandwich. Economy.

Mrs Stockmann (*smiling*) Are you implying that Thomas and I are decadents?

Mayor Not you. Never you. (*He points towards the Doctor's study.*) Is he in?

Mrs Stockmann No. He's taken the boys for a walk.

Mayor Is that advisable? So soon after eating?

A noise in the hall.

That's them, is it?

Mrs Stockmann I don't think that can be them yet.

A knock on the door.

Come in.

Hovstad, the editor of the local newspaper, walks in from the hall.

Oh. Mr Hovstad?

Hovstad Yes. I'm so sorry, I had to finish up at the press. Good evening, sir.

Mayor Good evening. Business with my brother, is it?

Hovstad Partly.

Mayor He's become the darling of *The People's Messenger*, hasn't he?

Hovstad He writes when he feels something ought to be said.

Mrs Stockmann indicates the dining room.

Mrs Stockmann Won't you . . . Please?

Mayor Yes. Well. He's writing to the converted, isn't he? I'm not saying that your newspaper is a bad one, Mr Hovstad –

Hovstad No? Thank you.

Mayor There's a tolerance here, a community spirit that I applaud. Because we have a strong communal interest. A mutual concern.

Hovstad The Baths?

Mayor Exactly. You can quote me on this, sir. Those Baths will prove the very lifeblood of our community. We've had a boom here over the past two or three years. The quality of life. Property's gone up, rents are higher.

Hovstad More jobs.

Mayor Yes. Absolutely. What we really need is proper invalids. They'd be a very good advertisement for the Baths.

Hovstad They say it's going to be a busy summer.

Mayor Every day. There's enquiries. About accommodation.

Hovstad The Doctor's article will be very timely, then.

Mayor He's written another one, has he?

Hovstad He wrote it last winter. About the Baths. I kept it back, though.

Mayor Something wrong with it?

Hovstad No. I just thought the spring was better timing with people planning their holidays here.

Mayor Well done, Mr Hovstad.

Mrs Stockmann Thomas's every thought lately is about the Baths.

Mayor It's his living.

Hovstad It was his brainchild, wasn't it?

Mayor Was it? Was it really? I've heard that opinion bandied about. I must say I laboured under the illusion that my contribution was no small part of the Baths coming into being.

Mrs Stockmann The Baths could never have happened without you. Thomas has always said that.

Hovstad No one would question that, sir. The funding. The construction. I only meant that it was the Doctor's idea. Originally.

Mayor Thomas has always had ideas, he's that way inclined. But when things have to be done, it requires a different sort of person, Mr Hovstad. And I would have thought that in this house especially it would be recognised that my contribution –

Mrs Stockmann Peter –

Hovstad I'm sorry, I didn't mean –

Mrs Stockmann Please, Mr Hovstad. Why don't you go in and join Mr Billing? Please. My husband will be home any minute.

Hovstad Thank you. I will.

Hovstad goes into the dining room.

Mayor That's the thing about folk without background. They never learn tact, do they?

Mrs Stockmann He didn't mean anything by it. You and Thomas are brothers, you must simply share the honours.

Mayor Quite. Only it seems not everyone's prepared to share.

Mrs Stockmann That's him, I think.

Mrs Stockmann crosses to the door to the hall and opens it. There are the sounds of small boys running up a couple of stairs and of a drum and trumpet being played badly by them. Stockmann is in the hall, laughing, boisterous.

Stockmann (*from the hall*) Hello, Catherine. Look who I bumped into just down the street? Come in, come in, Captain Horster. Give me your coat. Oh, you haven't got one. I practically had to kidnap him to get him back here into the warm.

Stockmann enters the room and shouts back to his sons.

Boys! Hands. Wash. Then in and eat. They're ravenous again, permanently hungry.

Captain Horster enters and shakes hands with Mrs Stockmann.

Now. Captain Horster, you are going to sample the finest roast beef you've ever . . .

Stockmann starts to corral Captain Horster towards the food.

Mrs Stockmann Thomas! Your brother . . .

Stockmann turns in the doorway.

Stockmann Oh. Hello, Peter.

He goes to the Mayor and shakes his hand.

It's good to see you.

Mayor I'm afraid I can't stay.

Stockmann Why not? Have a hot toddy.

Mrs Stockmann Yes do, the kettle's just boiling.

A trumpet sounds from the dining room. Mrs Stockmann looks into the dining room.

Eilif! Put it down. Morten, take your elbows off the table.

Mrs Stockmann goes into the dining room.

Stockmann Toddy?

Mayor Whisky and lemon, is it?

Stockmann Yes. Sit, and I'll get you one.

Mayor Thank you, no. I don't partake in drinking parties.

Stockmann It's not exactly a party.

Mayor Yes. Well, anyhow. (*He looks towards the dining room.*) Those boys. They'll eat you out of house and home.

Stockmann I hope they do. Young people should eat. They're more like bears than bear cubs. Which is as it should be. If they don't eat they don't grow. And if they don't grow, then there's no one to look out for the world when we've gone, is there? And that would be just grizz.

Mayor What do you mean by grizz?

Stockmann No idea. You'll have to ask Morten and Eilif. We can't see what the world needs, they'll see when the time comes. We're middle-aged. Dinosaurs.

Mayor Dinosaurs, is it?

Stockmann Don't look so serious, Pete. What? I just feel good – is that a crime? It's a wonderful time to be alive, isn't it? Everything feels like it's just on the edge of a fantastic explosion. It's all growing, blooming. It's as if a whole new age were being birthed in front of our very eyes.

Mayor Birthed?

Stockmann It's different for you. You've been here watching it all flower and evolve. You've witnessed the changes amassing. But I've been stuck. For years. In that stagnant backwater with the same old faces and their inane questions drilling a hole into my brain. I feel as though I've moved into an incredible metropolis.

Mayor Metropolis?

Stockmann People have a purpose here. There are things to really work and fight for. And that's all that matters in the end. (*Shouts.*) Catherine! Was there any post?

Mrs Stockmann (*from the dining room*) No.

Stockmann And to be able to support my family. Finally. It's fantastic. It was pretty grim, Peter. It's . . . it's very . . . good . . . here.

Mayor Come on now.

Stockmann Sorry, but it was – tough, bleak. Now we can live like kings. Do you like the tablecloth? I picked up that lamp too.

Mayor Yes. I noticed that.

Stockmann And the shade? It's all from what Catherine has managed to save. It's cosy, no? Come and stand here – no, not there. Here. Now look. You see how the light filters downwards at that angle? It's quite beautiful, don't you think?

Mayor If you like that sort of thing.

Stockmann I do. Catherine says I earn almost as much as I spend now.

Mayor Almost?

Stockmann A man of science needs a few aesthetic luxuries. I'm sure your average magistrate spends much more in a year than I do.

Mayor They can afford to.

Stockmann My only luxury is entertaining. I've always needed people around me, you know that. I've been in that godforsaken place for, Christ, for too long. I need to hear new ideas, opinions. Those men, and those boys in there, eating, laughing, they have lively wonderful minds. You should get to know Hovstad. He's quite incredible.

Mayor He said he's printing another of your –

Stockmann Articles. Is he?

Mayor About the Baths. From last winter.

Stockmann Oh that. No, I don't want them to print that any more.

Mayor Why not? It'd be good for trade.

Stockmann Yes. Normally it would.

Stockmann walks across the room. The Mayor watches him.

Mayor What do you mean? What is it?

Stockmann I can't say. Not yet. Not tonight, at any rate. Everything may be extraordinary, Peter. Or everything may be ordinary. It might all be a trick of the light.

Mayor Why are you being so mysterious? What can't you tell me? I'm Chairman of the Baths Committee – if anyone ought to know what's going on, it should be me.

Stockmann The Chairman yes. Chair. Man. Whilst I was . . . No, let's . . . forget it.

Pause.

Mayor Anything pertaining to matters in the town should be dealt with through the correct channels. Nothing underhand.

Stockmann When was I ever involved with something underhand?

Mayor It's just you've always done things . . . You were always different. You can't stay like that if you want to be part of the community – there's a system here. You've got to toe the line with the people. More specifically, with the authorities who are dealing with the public's good.

Stockmann The public's good? And what the hell has that got to do with me?

Mayor You see. You never change. Excuse me.

He bows towards the dining room.

Goodbye, Catherine. Good evening, gentlemen.

The Mayor leaves. Mrs Stockmann comes into the living room.

Mrs Stockmann Has he gone?

Stockmann Yes. God, he just can't bear it.

Mrs Stockmann Bear what? What did you say to him?

Stockmann Nothing. What? Are you sure there was no post?

Hovstad, Billing and Horster come into the living room. Billing stretches his arms.

Billing A meal like that makes one feel reborn!

Hovstad The Mayor seemed a bit . . . grizz.

Stockmann It's his digestion. He suffers from acid.

Hovstad I don't expect we radicals go down too well in his digestive tract.

Mrs Stockmann I thought you all got on.

Hovstad It's a temporary truce.

Billing Exactly. An ephemeral armistice.

Stockmann Peter's . . . very much on his own. He has no one to go home to, just work. And tea. Gallons of tea. Come on, then, let's relax. Is that toddy ready, Catherine?

Mrs Stockmann goes into the dining room.

Sit over here next to me, Horster. You never call. You should, you should. Sit, sit down.

The men sit at the table. Mrs Stockmann comes in with a tray on which is a kettle, decanters and glasses.

Mrs Stockmann So . . . this is arrack, rum, brandy. Tuck in.

Stockmann takes a glass.

Stockmann This is perfect. Where are the cigars?

Mrs Stockmann places them on the table.

I've a suspicion Eilif pinches a cigar once in a while, but I pretend not to notice. (*Shouts.*) Morten! Can you find me my smoking cap?

There follows a scuffle offstage with a few shouts while the others are talking.

Catherine, do you know where the tyke has left it? (*Indicating the cigars.*) Help yourselves, my friends. I'm a pipe man myself. This old pipe's been a port in many a storm up north.

He raises his glass.

Skol!

They clink their glasses. Mrs Stockmann takes up her knitting.

That's . . . This is really. Bliss.

Mrs Stockmann Will you be sailing soon, Captain Horster?

Horster We hope to set sail next week.

Mrs Stockmann To America?

Horster Yes. With God's grace.

Billing You won't get to vote in this coming council election.

Horster Is there one? I never vote.

Billing Oh, but you should, it's your right.

Horster Even if you don't understand what you're voting for?

Hovstad You sailors couldn't care less about what goes on on dry land, could you?

Billing It's very odd.

Stockmann Sailors are like migrating birds. Wherever they are, that's their home. Which means the home birds have to be all the more vigilant. So, Mr Hovstad, any gossip from tomorrow's *Messenger*?

Hovstad Nothing local. Your article's going in the day after tomorrow, though.

Stockmann Actually, you'll just have to sit on that one.

Hovstad Now's a good time for it.

Stockmann Yes. But you'll have to wait.

Petra enters from the hall. She wears a hat and cloak and carries a pile of exercise books.

Petra Hello.

Stockmann You're back, Petra. Hello.

The men greet Petra and she them. She takes off her cloak and hat and puts them and her books on a chair by the door.

Petra You've all been having a party while I've been out edifying the next generation.

Stockmann Come and join the bacchanalian orgy then, Miss.

Mrs Stockmann Thomas.

Billing Drink?

Petra comes over to the table.

Petra I'll do it. You make it so strong. I've a letter for you, Father.

Petra crosses back to her cloak and books.

Stockmann From the school? What have I done? Have I been naughty?

Petra looks in her pocket.

Petra The postman gave it to me just as I was leaving this morning.

Stockmann gets up and goes over to her.

Stockmann This morning? Why didn't you say so? Why didn't you tell me?

Petra I just did. I'm sorry. I just . . . I didn't have time to run back with it.

Petra produces the letter, Stockmann seizes it.

Stockmann Give it to me. Let me see it.

He inspects the envelope.

Yes. This is it. Right.

Mrs Stockmann Is it what you've been waiting for, Thomas?

Stockmann Yes. Yes. I'll just go . . . I need to . . . I'll be in the study. Don't let the boys run in.

Mrs Stockmann I won't.

Stockmann Excuse me a moment.

He goes into his study.

Petra What is it?

Mrs Stockmann I don't know. He's been waiting for it in a fever for the past week.

Petra He's been working like a maniac this last few months.

Mrs Stockmann Petra.

Petra What? (*She drinks.*) Oh that's good.

Hovstad Were you at your evening classes tonight?

Petra Yes.

Billing And four hours teaching.

Petra sits at the table.

Petra Five.

Mrs Stockmann And you've brought all of those back with you?

Petra They need marking.

Horster It seems like your father's not the only one who's –

Hovstad – working like a maniac.

Petra I like it. I like the feeling of being so ecstatically tired you could drop.

Billing Ecstatically?

Petra Yes. You sleep very soundly after falling from such a high desk.

Billing You must be very wicked.

Petra Wicked?

Billing My old teacher said work was a punishment for our sins.

Petra Perhaps I am. My little brother Eilif is a heathen, you know.

Mrs Stockmann Rubbish.

Petra He told Morten he wanted to be a Viking and Morten said he'd have to be a heathen to become one, so now he's resolved to give up religion.

Mrs Stockmann Petra . . .

Billing I'm with him there. Tell your little brother that's just the way I feel.

Mrs Stockmann You're being ironic, Mr Billing.

Billing I assure you I'm not. I'm a heathen. And proud. Before long we'll all jump ship.

Petra And lead a life of unmitigated pleasure?

Mrs Stockmann Petra. Darling.

Petra Mother. We're just talking.

Mrs Stockmann I don't like that sort of talk. Not here. In the home.

Petra Everyone's terrified of the truth. I have to censor myself in my own home and I have to preach lies to the children at school.

Horster You lie to them?

Petra I'm paid to teach them things I don't believe in myself.

Billing Bureaucracy, you see.

Petra If I had the money I'd start my own school. I'd do things very differently.

Billing Money, yes. Ghastly money.

Horster If you're serious about it, Miss Stockmann, if it's simply space you need, you'd be welcome at my late father's house. There's a huge dining room downstairs going to waste.

Petra laughs.

Petra Thank you. But I don't suppose I'll really do it.

Hovstad I think you should seriously consider journalism, Miss Petra. Have you read that novel you were going to translate for us?

Petra I haven't. But don't worry. I'll get your draft in on time.

Stockmann enters from his room with the letter open in his hand. He waves it.

Stockmann News! Incredible news! It's . . . it's . . .

Billing Where's the fire?

Mrs Stockmann What is it, Tom?

Stockmann A great discovery has been made, Catherine.

Mrs Stockmann About what? Who's discovered what?

Stockmann Now let them tell me I'm imagining things. Voices in my head? Yes? Really? They'll have to be very careful now. (*He laughs.*) Yes. Very. Very. Careful.

Petra What's going on, Pa?

Stockmann Give me a moment. One moment. God, I wish Peter was here. It just goes to show how blind people can be.

Hovstad Who is blind, Doctor?

Stockmann This town purports to be a place of infinite health, doesn't it?

Hovstad It's a spa.

Stockmann Exactly. Actively brilliant for those who are infirm or even for those who are not but seek the wonders of the waters, yes?

Mrs Stockmann Yes. Thomas. Please.

Stockmann And we ourselves have placed it on a pedestal, have we not? I've written eulogies, thousands of words of copy about its benefits, haven't I?

Hovstad Yes. Yes you have.

Stockmann These Baths my friends, these Baths which have been coined the artery of the town, the central nervous system, the –

Billing 'The pulsating heart of our idyllic town', I once called them, after one particularly boozy lunchtime.

Stockmann Do you know what they really are, these beloved Baths of ours into which we've poured our blood and money? Do you know what they are?

Hovstad What are they?

Stockmann They're nothing but a damned cesspit.

Petra The Baths, Pa?

Mrs Stockmann (*simultaneously*) Our Baths!

Hovstad (*simultaneously*) But Doctor . . .

Billing What do you mean?

Stockmann These Baths are a contaminated death trap. They are a health hazard of the highest degree. All of that filth up at Moelledal – you know, all the stinking refuse and scum from the tanneries – it's all filtered through to the water in the pump-room pipes. It's contaminated them. And it's infected the Seaweed Baths, too. The whole place is toxic.

Hovstad Where has all this come from?

Stockmann I've been studying it for a while now. I knew that something was wrong. Last year there was an abnormal number of typhoid cases amongst the visitors. And gastric troubles.

Mrs Stockmann I remember.

Stockmann We thought they'd simply brought their illnesses with them. But then I started seeing holes in that theory. I've been analysing the waters. As far as I've been able to.

Mrs Stockmann That's what you've been working on these past months.

Stockmann Yes. But I've no real kit as such. So I sent specimens of the fresh and salt water to the University laboratories.

Hovstad And they've come back to you about it?

Stockmann It's all here. It establishes conclusively that the water is riddled with toxins, millions of bacteria. It's dangerous to wash in, let alone drink.

Mrs Stockmann Thank God you found out.

Stockmann Yes.

Hovstad What can they do about it?

Stockmann I think I know how we can put it right.

Mrs Stockmann Why didn't you say something? Why did you keep this whole thing to yourself?

Stockmann Should I have taken Eilif's trumpet around town and gathered people together to hear the local mad scientist before I had solid evidence? No.

Petra But us, Pa, you might have told us.

Stockmann Tomorrow. You can race along to the old Badger and . . .

Mrs Stockmann Thomas.

Stockmann Sorry. Your father. He thinks I'm mental, you know. Him and all the rest. It's going to be chaos, Catherine. Carnage. Do you see what they're going to have to do? They're going to have to re-lay every single water pipe.

Hovstad The whole system?

Stockmann It has to be done. They started the intake too low down the hill. They've got to reroute the whole mess a few feet higher.

Petra Which is what you said in the first place.

Stockmann You remember? I did. I petitioned against the original plans. But they all refused to listen. I've written a full report for the Baths Committee. It's been sat on my desk for a week now, just waiting for confirmation.

He goes into his study and returns with a sheaf of papers.

Here it is. Ten pages, single spacing. I'll put the results in with it. Have we got a newspaper Catherine?

Mrs Stockmann hands him a newspaper. He wraps the letter and results in it.

Good. There. Now. Give it to . . . to . . . I can never remember her name? The maid. Tell her to take it to my brother's. To leave whatever she's doing. Yes?

Mrs Stockmann takes the parcel, and leaves through the dining room.

Petra What do you think Uncle Peter will say, Pa?

Stockmann What is there to say? He'll be very glad that it's come to light.

Hovstad I could put a notice in the *Messenger*.

Stockmann That would be useful. Very useful.

Hovstad People should know about this as soon as possible.

Stockmann Absolutely. Yes.

Mrs Stockmann enters.

Mrs Stockmann I gave it to her. She's gone.

Billing You'll be the man of the match, Doctor, a local hero.

Stockmann I'm only doing my work. I dug for treasure. And I found it. Nothing more. Still . . . still . . .

Billing Hovstad, we should have a torchlit procession in honour of the Doctor.

Hovstad Absolutely. Do it.

Billing I'll get Aslaksen onto it.

Stockmann No. Please. My friends. No fuss. Nothing like that. And if the Baths Committee offer me a raise, I'll just say no. No. No.

Mrs Stockmann You're a good man, Thomas.

Petra (*raising her glass*) Skol, Pa!

Hovstad/Billing/Horster Skol!

Horster (*clinks with the Doctor*) Here's wishing you joy. Nothing but joy with your new discovery!

Stockmann Thank you, my dear friends. Thank you. I'm deeply . . . To have the respect of one's fellow men, it's . . . Eh, Catherine? It's beautiful, isn't it? Isn't it?

Stockmann puts his arms around her waist, then he picks her up. She screams and giggles. Laughter, applause, cheers for the Doctor. The boys play their trumpet and drum offstage.

Act Two

The living room. Morning. The door to the dining room is shut.
    Mrs Stockmann enters from the dining room with a sealed letter in her hand. She goes to the study door and looks in.

Mrs Stockmann You're here.

Stockmann (*from the study*) Yes. I've just got in.

    Stockmann walks into the living room.

Mrs Stockmann It's from Peter.

    She gives him the letter.

Stockmann Ah. What does he say?

    He opens the envelope.

'I return herewith the manuscript you sent me –' (*Reads on, mumbles.*) Hmm.

Mrs Stockmann What?

    He puts the letter in his pocket.

Stockmann He'll be here at noon.

Mrs Stockmann Good. And you're not going out again? You've finished your rounds?

Stockmann I have.

Mrs Stockmann How do you think he'll take it?

Stockmann He won't like it. That I made the discovery and not him.

Mrs Stockmann Tom . . .

Stockmann Don't worry. Peter hates anyone doing good for the town other than himself. But he will be delighted. Deep down.

Mrs Stockmann Perhaps you should say you discovered it together? That it was he who suggested you carry out the research?

Stockmann Listen, as long as we can fix it. I don't care who takes the credit.

Old Morten Kiil puts his head through the door leading from the hall. He looks around enquiringly. He laughs to himself.

Morten Is it . . . is it true?

Stockmann Morten Kiil, hello. Good morning, good morning.

Mrs Stockmann Are you coming in or not, Father?

Morten I am if it's true.

Stockmann If what's true?

Morten This wonderful fiction about the water system. Is it true, eh?

Stockmann It's all true. Who have you been talking to?

Morten Kiil comes in.

Morten Petra came by on her way to the school.

Stockmann Did she now? That was very thoughtful of her.

Morten Told me all about it. I thought she was joking me. Winding me round her little finger.

Stockmann Why would she want to do that?

Morten Trust no one. You get led down a blind alley before you know you're there. It's true, what she said?

Stockmann It is. Come and sit down.

He indicates the sofa, Morten Kiil sits.

It's a good job for everyone that it's all come out, isn't it?

Morten Kiil tries not to laugh.

Morten A good job!

Stockmann That I found out sooner rather than later.

Morten Absolutely, absolutely. So you're playing monkey tricks on your brother.

Stockmann Monkey tricks?

Mrs Stockmann Pa, darling . . .

Morten What was it? Animals are swimming around the pipes?

Stockmann Bacteria, yes.

Morten Masses of them, Petra says. Battalions of bacteria lashing and splashing around.

Stockmann Millions. yes.

Morten But you can't see any of them, can you?

Stockmann No, they're invisible to the naked eye.

Morten You've finally developed a sense of humour, my boy.

Stockmann What?

Morten You won't fool the Mayor, though. He's not a child.

Stockmann I'm hoping the whole town will be children if it takes a child to believe it.

Morten You're going to tell everybody? Good. Teach them all a lesson. They hounded me off that Council as if I were a dog. You go ahead and play monkey tricks on them, Stockmann!

Stockmann Listen. Father . . .

Morten Do it! Monkey tricks. (*He gets up.*) If you can put the Council's nose out of joint I'll write a cheque for a hundred crowns and send it to the workhouse today.

Stockmann That's very kind.

Morten I'm not rich, but if you harangue those bastards I'll give fifty crowns to the homeless Christmas dinner.

Hovstad comes in from the hall.

Hovstad Good morning. Oh, sorry. Should I come back in a bit?

Stockmann No, no. Come in.

Morten Is he in on this, too?

Hovstad I'm sorry?

Stockmann He is, yes.

Morten Unbelievable. You're going to print it all up? I take my hat off to you, Stockmann. I really do. I'm off. You two, yes, get on with it, get on with it.

Stockmann You only just got here.

Morten Nevertheless. Every trick in the book, mind. I'll see you right.

Mrs Stockmann walks her father out.

Stockmann He doesn't believe a single word of it. The bacteria, the pipes.

Hovstad Oh, that's what he was talking about. Listen, do you have a moment?

Stockmann Of course.

Hovstad Have you heard back from your brother?

Stockmann He's coming over later.

Hovstad I've been thinking.

Stockmann I won't tell anyone.

Hovstad What? (*He gets the joke. Smiles.*) It's just . . . you're a man of science. You think of all this technically. It's a chemical problem. The thing is, you don't see the wider implications . . .

Stockmann I'm not quite with you.

They sit down, Hovstad on the sofa, Stockmann in an armchair.

Hovstad You said the source of the pollution was impurity in the soil.

Stockmann Yes. It originates in the swamp at Moelledal.

Hovstad Right. Well, I believe the true origin of it is elsewhere.

Stockmann Where?

Hovstad It's the infested swamp in which our whole community is quietly rotting.

Stockmann You're speaking metaphorically?

Hovstad Little by little this whole town has fallen into the hands of an exclusive clique of bureaucratic civil servants.

Stockmann They're not all civil servants.

Hovstad Those who aren't hang on to the tails of those who are. Basically it's the rich old money, and they dictate to us.

Stockmann There are some intelligent men in that crowd. Astute men.

Hovstad Who was being astute when they laid down the system? They sited the pipes so low that they've polluted the whole town. Was that intelligent?

Stockmann No, that was stupid. But we're fixing that.

Hovstad Are we?

Stockmann Yes, of course we are.

Hovstad If the press has its way, then yes, we'll repair the damage.

Stockmann It's not a question of the press. My brother will –

Hovstad I intend to shout about it.

Stockmann In print?

Hovstad When I took over this paper it was because I wanted to break up this ring of ancient bigots.

Stockmann When you attacked them you were almost forced to shut up shop.

Hovstad We had to be on the back foot for a while. If the men we'd targeted had been run out of office the Baths would never have been built. But now their money's secure. It's in the fabric of the buildings. In the bricks. We don't need to be nice to them any more.

Stockmann We still owe them some sort of gratitude.

Hovstad Possibly. But I set up my paper to tell the truth, not to kowtow to whoever happens to be rich. I'm going to destroy the myth of their brilliance. I'm going to smash their reputations down like hollow rotten trees.

Stockmann If there's rot, it must be attended to.

Hovstad I don't want to involve your brother. If I could avoid that I would. I really would. But we're talking about something bigger than blood, aren't we? You. Me. We seek the truth don't we, above everything else?

Stockmann We do. We do. But . . . well . . .

Hovstad I'm only doing what's right. I'm no more ambitious or self-seeking than the next man.

Stockmann I know that.

Hovstad I grew up with nothing. I know what the poor need. It's to have a say in local affairs. A voice. That's the way towards achieving something better, freedom. It's the path to knowledge, dignity.

Stockmann I agree.

Hovstad A journalist neglects his mission if he ignores an opportunity to achieve emancipation for the oppressed. The fat cats will call me a demagogue. I don't care. My conscience is clear.

Stockmann Absolutely. I couldn't agree with you more. But still . . . .

A knock at the door.

Come in.

Aslaksen, the printer, appears in the door leading from the hall. He is modestly but decently dressed in black, with a white, slightly crumpled cravat and gloves, and carries a silk hat. He bows.

Aslaksen I hope you'll forgive the intrusion, Doctor.

Stockmann gets up.

Stockmann Hello. You're the printer aren't you, Mr Aslaksen?

35

Aslaksen I am, sir.

Hovstad gets up.

Hovstad Did you need me, Aslaksen?

Aslaksen No, no, sir. Point of fact I had no idea you was here. No. It was the Doctor I wanted to . . .

Stockmann What can I do for you?

Aslaksen I just wondered if it was true, sir, what I heard from Mr Billing, about you wanting to improve the water system?

Stockmann Yes, it is.

Aslaksen Oh. Well I just came round to offer my support, Doctor.

Hovstad You see.

Stockmann Thank you. I'm not quite . . .

Aslaksen Just you might find it helpful. Having tradesmen behind you. We're a pretty strong force when we have a mind to get together. Always good to have the majority behind you, Doctor.

Stockmann Thank you. Yes. But in this case everything's pretty straightforward. So I don't see that I'll need it.

Aslaksen As you say, sir, but you still might need a hand. I've had dealings with the Council. They hate anything coming in from the outside. I thought we might have a little picket.

Hovstad It's a good idea.

Stockmann A what? What are we picketing against?

Aslaksen I'm not talking about a riot, sir. Just a quiet show of feeling. Restraint is a wonderful thing, Doctor.

Stockmann Yes. I've heard about your love of restraint.

Aslaksen This water issue, it's vital to us, you see. We're sitting on a cash cow with the Baths. They'll be our income from now on in, especially the home-owners. So, as I say, we're with you all the way, Doctor. Also you see I'm Chairman of the Property Owners' Association.

Stockmann Ah. I see.

Aslaksen And I'm on the Board of the Temperance Society. You knew I was a temperance worker, did you?

Stockmann Yes. Yes.

Aslaksen My point being, I come into contact with a lot of people. I'm well-liked. My say-so is often seen as a temperature gauge for the rest of the people. All I'm saying is, I could arrange an address if you needed one. A vote of thanks. From the people of the town. Course I can't go overboard with it or the powers-that-be will get the hump, won't they?

Hovstad I wouldn't bother about them.

Aslaksen We must, Mr Hovstad. We can't afford to offend the authorities. They're our bread and butter. I've seen plenty of that in my time and it's all blood and shit, pardon my language. But a quiet show of support, well, no man can be denied that privilege, can he?

Stockmann (*shaking his hand*) My dear Aslaksen, I am really touched. I am. Really touched. Can I get you a sherry?

Aslaksen Oh, no no. I never touch spirits.

Stockmann A glass of beer, then? Just the one?

Aslaksen No. Thank you, Doctor. It's a bit early in the day for me. I should get back. Lay the ground for all of this.

Stockmann It's terribly kind of you, Mr Aslaksen. But I hate to think of you wasting your time. I really think the matter will resolve itself very simply.

Aslaksen Bureaucracy works very slowly here, Doctor. Don't quote me on that.

Hovstad We'll start rousing the rabble in tomorrow's paper, Aslaksen.

Aslaksen As long as you proceed with moderation, Mr Hovstad. Restraint. Otherwise you're on a trip to nowhere. I've seen it all, me, and it's not very clever. Cheerio then. You know now. We're behind you, Doctor. Like a wall. Solid. United.

Stockmann (*shakes his hand*) Thank you, Mr Aslaksen. Goodbye.

Aslaksen Are you coming back with me, Mr Hovstad?

Hovstad I'll be down in a while. I've a few things to attend to.

Aslaksen Yes. Good. Right. Well then.

Aslaksen bows and goes out. Stockmann sees him out into the hall, then walks back in.

Hovstad You see what I mean? Everyone in this town has mislaid a backbone.

Stockmann Aslaksen?

Hovstad Aslaksen. All of them. He's all right, but he's an invertebrate along with all the others in this liberal-minded swamp. They're all so damned stagnant.

Stockmann He seems decent enough.

Hovstad Decent. You've got to have courage. The courage of your own convictions. Know your own mind. I want to get these men to stand up for themselves. To stop doffing their damn caps to the bosses. The Baths are endangering people's lives for profit. And the people have a right to know.

Stockmann Let me talk to my brother first.

Hovstad I'll prep the editorial. And if the Mayor's response is in any way obstructive . . .

Stockmann It won't be.

Hovstad What's your plan if he doesn't co-operate?

Stockmann He will. If he opposes immediate action even for a moment, then you can print the whole of my report. Whenever it suits you.

Hovstad You'd let me do that? Do you give me your word?

Stockmann gives the manuscript to Hovstad.

Stockmann There. It's yours. You'll be giving it back to me before you've even had a chance to read it.

Hovstad I hope so. Goodbye, Doctor.

Stockmann Goodbye. Hovstad, this will all be sorted. Very simply. Really.

Hovstad Courage. That's all we need.

Hovstad nods and goes out through the hall.
Stockmann goes over to the dining room and looks in.

Stockmann Catherine! Oh, hello, Petra. I didn't know you were here.

Petra enters.

Petra I just got back.

Mrs Stockmann enters.

Mrs Stockmann He's not here yet?

Stockmann No. I just had a chat with Hovstad. He's very excited about it all. He says the newspaper's at my disposal should I need it.

Mrs Stockmann Why would you?

Stockmann No reason. But it's always good to have the press on your side. And then the Chairman of the . . . the Property Owners' Association was here. Do you realise what I have behind me, Catherine?

Mrs Stockmann What?

Stockmann The solid majority.

Mrs Stockmann And that's good, is it?

A doorbell rings.

That'll be him.

A knock on the inner door.

Come in.

The Mayor enters from the hall.

Mayor Good morning.

Stockmann (*warmly*) Hello, Peter.

Mrs Stockmann Good morning, Peter. How are you?

Mayor Adequate. Thank you. Late last night I received your . . . communication. About the Baths.

Stockmann Have you read it yet?

Mayor I have.

Stockmann And . . .

Mayor I . . . I . . .

He looks at the women.

Mrs Stockmann Petra.

The women go into the room on the left. Pause.

Mayor It's been over a year since you started probing into this. You didn't think to discuss it with me?

Stockmann I wanted to be sure of the facts.

Mayor And now you are?

Stockmann You've read them.

Mayor And you propose to give the results and your statement to the Baths Committee?

Stockmann Yes. They've got to do something about it. Immediately.

Mayor (*quoting from the report*) 'All we can offer our visitors at present is the promise of poisoning, paralysis and pestilence.' Very good use of alliteration for dramatic effect.

Stockmann It's fact not drama. The waters are toxic. People who are already sick are bathing in them, they're giving us their savings as well as their faith in the hope of a cure. They're drinking it, for Christ's sake.

Mayor You recommend we drain the whole of the Moelledal swamp and then reroute the miles of water pipes.

Stockmann It's got to be done.

Mayor I saw the town engineer this morning. I sounded him out gently about possible future work.

Stockmann Now, Peter. It's got to be now.

Mayor He smiled at me as if I were a lunatic. Do you have any idea how much we're talking here? A starting cost of several hundred thousand crowns.

Stockmann Really? That much?

Mayor Two years we're talking about.

Stockmann No? Surely they can fix it quicker than that.

Mayor Two years minimum. Meantime, what do we do? We close the Baths. We'd have no choice. Not a soul would come here anyway if a word of this filtered out.

Stockmann I don't see an alternative, do you?

Mayor Everyone who's booked to come here will stay at the neighbouring towns instead. They'll cash in on our lost trade. Our repairs budget will doubtless dry up halfway through reconstruction. Basically, you intend to cripple this town.

Stockmann I? Cripple . . .

Mayor Our only revenue is as a spa town. So you tell me now, how will we survive?

Stockmann I don't see what else we can do.

Mayor I think you're exaggerating the situation.

Stockmann If anything I'm underplaying it. Once the summer comes, it'll be a hotbed of disease.

Mayor The established water supply to the Baths is now a fact and must be treated as such. I expect the Committee can be persuaded to make a few gradual improvements.

Stockmann No. No! It's got to be a complete overhaul. You can't hush this up, Peter.

Mayor Hush what up?

Stockmann Don't. Don't do that. You know me. I can't play along with . . . lies.

Mayor Lies?

Stockmann Council propaganda. Veiling the facts.

Mayor But I just told you. I'm not convinced there's actual danger.

Stockmann Really? You don't think that these results, which state plainly that the water is toxic . . . you don't think they point to a critical situation?

Mayor No.

Stockmann And you're sure, of course you're sure, that it's not another aspect of this that's actually worrying you? It's not the fact that it was you who chose the original site? You dictated where to lay the pipes. You refused to lay them where I advised you to. And now you're terrified of looking incompetent. Inept.

Mayor I am the moral guardian of this town. People look to me for . . . You cannot give your report to the Baths Committee. It has to be suppressed. For the general good. I will bring it to their attention. And we will discuss it. But all in good time. And discreetly. And we will see what can be done about it. Nothing – not one word of this – can go further than these four walls.

Stockmann The wheels are in motion, Peter.

Mayor Not a word, Thomas.

Stockmann It's too late. People know.

Mayor Which people? You don't mean Hovstad and his shower?

Stockmann You can't silence a whole newspaper.

Pause.

Mayor You never were very bright, Tom. You don't see the hole you've dug for yourself, do you?

Stockmann I don't see any hole. Show me it.

Mayor It's a gaping great hole. Big enough for you. Your wife. Your three children.

Stockmann What are you saying?

Mayor I've helped you. Haven't I?

Stockmann And I've been grateful.

Mayor I don't want your gratitude. It's been as much for my sake as yours. Do you think someone in my position can afford to be associated with scandal?

Stockmann You think I'm scandalous?

Mayor You invite controversy.

Stockmann I don't.

Mayor You do. You have to shout and write about every new idea or complaint you have. You've got to read about your own anger in the paper before you can truly feel it.

Stockmann It's my duty to share what I feel with the public.

Mayor You've always been a selfish bastard. Who got you that job at the Baths?

Stockmann There wouldn't have been any Baths if I hadn't seen that this was the perfect climate for a spa town. I pushed the idea for years. I wrote about it. Pages! Pages of bloody reports I wrote!

Mayor You weren't even resident here. We were here. We knew when the time was ripe for it.

Stockmann And then you mucked it all up. You and your brilliant bloody associates!

Mayor You're aching for a fight, aren't you? You never could take authority, could you? I've told you what's at stake. And I'm not about to compromise.

Stockmann So what will you do?

Mayor You've been stupid enough to . . . You're just going to have to retract the whole thing. Publicly.

Stockmann What did you just say?

Mayor You're going to find that you've been mistaken.

Stockmann Am I?

Mayor You'll express your confidence in the Committee and its commitment to ongoing improvements which may be merely cosmetic.

Stockmann You have to reroute the whole system, Peter!

Mayor As an employee you haven't the right to tell me anything . . .

Stockmann I haven't the right?

Mayor No. You work for me, Thomas. And you'll find, in your contract, that one of the rules is that you're not allowed to contradict a superior.

Stockmann What? I'm a Doctor, I'm a man of science, not a bloody –

Mayor The world doesn't revolve around your science! It's about money!

Stockmann Shit on your money! I never asked for your handouts! I'm free to express myself wherever I am.

Mayor Go on! You can say whatever you want! But you say one more word about the Baths – you talk about them outside of this house, and I'll . . .

Stockmann And you'll what? What?

Mayor I forbid you! I'm in charge of you! And what I say goes!

Stockmann Christ, Peter. If you weren't my brother . . .!

Petra throws open the door.

Petra Pa! Don't let him talk to you like that!

Mrs Stockmann follows her.

Mrs Stockmann Petra! Petra!

Mayor Ha! Spies!

Mrs Stockmann We'd need to be deaf not to hear you.

Petra I heard you. I could quote every word.

Mayor Good. Good!

Stockmann You were ordering me about like a dog.

Mayor You push me. You really do.

Stockmann And you expect me to deny the whole thing?

Mayor It's not negotiable.

Stockmann And if I refuse?

Mayor We'll counter your report with our own.

Stockmann I counter your riposte with my own. Then where do we stand?

Mayor Then . . . then you will be given your dismissal.

Stockmann What?

Petra Pa! Your job!

Mrs Stockmann You'd . . . Dismissal?

Mayor You'd be immediately released from your post as Public Medical Officer. And we would issue a restraint order to prevent your being in the vicinity of the Baths.

Stockmann A what?

Mayor Your behaviour makes it necessary.

Petra Uncle, you can't do this to Pa. You just can't.

Mrs Stockmann Not now, Petra.

Mayor So you've an opinion on it too, have you? Of course you do. Catherine, you're the only one in this house who exhibits any vestige of common sense. Talk to your husband. This affects all of you.

Stockmann You leave my bloody family out of this!

Mayor You are putting your family and your town at risk of destitution, Thomas.

Stockmann I love this town. That's why I'm doing this. I was born here.

Mayor And you'd stand by and see its heart dry up and die?

Stockmann Its heart is infected. Are you out of your mind, Peter? We're selling filth, trading disease. We're gaining sustenance from one huge deadly lie!

Mayor The man who says such a thing is a traitor to society.

Stockmann What did you call me?

Mrs Stockmann Thomas!

Petra Pa! Please! Pa!

Mayor You'd like to hit me, wouldn't you? I've said my piece. I'll leave you now. To consider your wife. And Petra. And Eilif. And Morten. Goodbye.

The Mayor leaves. Stockmann walks up and down.

Stockmann In my own house . . . Christ, Catherine!

Mrs Stockmann I know, Thomas. It's horrible.

Petra I wish I was a man.

Stockmann He called me a traitor. He's going to regret that.

Mrs Stockmann Thomas, darling, he's got everyone behind him.

Stockmann But I have truth and honour on my side.

Mrs Stockmann What good are they when you have no power?

Petra Mother, how can you say that?

Stockmann Just you watch, Catherine. I'm going to fight this battle to the death.

Mrs Stockmann He's threatening you with dismissal!

Petra Mother, you can't just think in terms of the family.

Mrs Stockmann You can make your own living! What about the boys, Thomas? And me? What about us?

Stockmann Catherine, if I give in to Peter, I would despair for the rest of my life.

Mrs Stockmann And what about the boys' despair when there's no food to eat? We've been there before, Thomas. For years. For the first time we're . . . You can't forget it all so quickly.

Stockmann Bureaucrats and lackeys. Endeavouring to shackle a free man. It's abhorrent, isn't it, Catherine?

Mrs Stockmann It is. It is. But people are abhorrent. The world is not a . . . The boys, Thomas! Thomas? The boys!

Stockmann Are my sons. And I am their father.

He walks towards his study.

Mrs Stockmann What will you do?

Stockmann I want to be able to look my sons in the eye when they grow up into free men.

He goes into the study. Mrs Stockmann bursts into tears.

Mrs Stockmann Oh God. Oh God. Help us. For God's sake.

Petra Father's right, Mother. Please. Mother.

Petra stands. Mrs Stockmann breaks down.

Act Three

The editorial office of The People's Messenger. *In the middle of the room is a large table covered with papers, books, newspapers. There are two armchairs by it and other chairs along the walls. Downstage left is a window and next to it is a writing desk and a high stool. The room is unkempt and bleak, the furniture is shabby, the armchairs dirty and torn. At the back on the left is the entrance from outside, to the right of that is the printing office with glass windows. One or two compositors are at work there. Beyond them a hand press is being operated. On the right-hand wall there is another door.*

Hovstad sits writing at the desk. Billing enters from the right with Stockmann's manuscript in his hand.

Billing Well! There it is.

Hovstad You read it?

Billing puts it down on the desk.

Billing It's . . .

Hovstad It's pretty strong stuff, isn't it?

Billing It's brilliant. Inflammatory. He lays into them like a bloody sledgehammer.

Hovstad They'll put up a fight.

Billing Then we just keep jabbing them. A sharp hook from the left which they're not expecting and they're down. I had a strong feeling reading it. This is what we've been waiting for, you know? It's the revolution.

Hovstad puts his finger to his lips, then indicates the office.

Hovstad Aslaksen.

Billing The man's a mollusc. You are going to publish this, aren't you?

Hovstad Unless the Mayor backs down.

Billing We'll have to pray that he doesn't.

Hovstad We're in whichever way he goes. If he opposes the article he'll have the tradesmen onto him. If he agrees to fix things he'll have the Baths Committee screaming down his back.

Billing It'll cost them thousands.

Hovstad Hundreds of thousands. Nothing like forking out money to break up a little clique. And then we go to work on the people. Tell them that the Mayor is incompetent. That the power should be with the liberals, not a posse of spineless bureaucrats.

Billing It's exciting, Hov. It really is. It feels like a bloody revolution.

A knock on the door.

Hovstad Try not to be so vocal about it, Billing. (*Shouts.*) Come in!

Stockmann enters from outside. Hovstad goes to greet him.

Hovstad It's you, Doctor. What did he say?

Stockmann Print it, Mr Hovstad.

Hovstad He refused to fix it?

Billing Fantastic!

Stockmann Print it in full. He rejects the whole thing. If he wants to play dirty, that's his choice. It's war now, Mr Billing.

Billing A fight to the death. You'll kill them, Doctor.

Stockmann This report is just the beginning. I've four or five more pieces I want printed after this one. Where's Aslaksen?

Billing calls into the office.

Billing Aslaksen! We need you here. Please. Mr Aslaksen?

Hovstad You're going to write follow-up articles?

Stockmann Not just about the Baths. But it's all related. You start to pull down a building, it all goes back to the foundations.

Billing And then you realise you have to put dynamite under the whole thing to do any good.

Aslaksen (*from the office*) Who's using dynamite?

Hovstad Nobody.

Aslaksen enters.

Stockmann Nothing explosive, Mr Aslaksen! What do you think of the report?

Hovstad It's brilliant, absolutely brilliant.

Stockmann Really? You think so? Thank you. That's . . . very nice to . . . Thank you.

Hovstad It's succinct without being spare. Brilliant. And it's so clear that anyone can follow the thrust of it. Every educated reader will be on your side.

Aslaksen The others too, I hope. Let's line it up then. For tomorrow's first edition.

Stockmann Mr Aslaksen, would you set this up yourself, please? We can't risk a single misprint. I could come back later. And proof-read it? It's going in tomorrow's, is it?

Billing Yes. It's just like a bomb, waiting to explode.

Aslaksen Mr Billing –

Stockmann I'm sorry if I'm a bit . . . I had a run in earlier with . . . My very rights as a human being were under fire.

Billing Your human rights?

Stockmann He ordered me to put my private concerns above my ideological beliefs.

Hovstad It doesn't surprise me.

Stockmann I'll fight him with words. On a daily basis. if needs be. The *Messenger* had better be armed for battle . . .

Aslaksen You have to remember –

Billing War! Tooth and nail!

Stockmann I'll beat their clique to a pulp. People will see them for what they really are.

Aslaksen Moderation, Doctor. Restraint is the key.

Billing To hell with restraint!

Stockmann It's not just the water any more. It's the moral fibre of the whole town. It has to be cleansed. Decontaminated.

Billing Bleached!

Stockmann We've got to bring in a whole new leadership. Young. Without cynicism.

Billing You're right! New blood!

Stockmann The key is unity.

Aslaksen As long as we exercise restraint. Then we'll steer clear of any dangerous corners.

Stockmann Bugger the danger! I'm talking about truth. Conscience.

Hovstad You're a unique man, Doctor.

Aslaksen A true citizen.

Billing A friend to the people!

Stockmann Thank you, my friends. It's like manna to my soul to hear you say that. My brother used quite a different turn of phrase. I've got to see a patient now. I'll be back. Don't let anyone get their hands on that, Aslaksen. And don't make any executive choices about the punctuation. Every single exclamation mark stays. If in doubt, add more. Good. Good. Goodbye.

He shakes hands with them as they accompany him to the door and he leaves.

Hovstad He's going to be bloody useful to us.

Aslaksen As long as he sticks to the Baths. If he goes off on his own parade we'll have to drop him.

Hovstad Not necessarily.

Billing What are you so scared of?

Aslaksen The local authorities. They're bloody terrifying. Give me a pop at the government I'd be fine, but this lot –

Billing You're a funny one.

Aslaksen You have a go at the government, nothing actually changes, does it? Get rid of this lot and you've got it all on your front doorstep. Some young idiot takes over, you can lose your house – anything might happen.

Hovstad I thought you believed in the working people and their self-government?

Aslaksen I also have a whimsical notion to keep a roof over my head.

Hovstad God preserve me and keep me away from the tyranny of the property ladder.

Billing Far from the mental shackles of mortgage payments.

Hovstad Shoot me if I ever become a conformist.

Aslaksen You've applied for that job as a secretary to the magistrate – that's not exactly radical, is it?

Billing I . . .

Hovstad You didn't? Did you?

Billing Only to annoy them.

Aslaksen I'm not apologising. My politics have always been left and I've never shifted on that front. But I do favour restraint when it comes to the local authorities. That's me.

Aslaksen exits into the printing office.

Billing Couldn't we get a different printer, Hov?

Hovstad Who else would do it for us on tick?

Billing We need money. Ghastly capital.

Hovstad Yes.

Billing What about Stockmann?

Hovstad (*glancing through his papers*) The Doctor? He hasn't got a penny.

Billing Morten Kiil has, though. The Badger's absolutely loaded.

Hovstad Urban myth.

Billing It's not, you know. He's as rich as Croesus. And it'll all go to the Stockmanns, won't it?

Hovstad You've worked it all out?

Billing I haven't graphed it. I haven't done the sums. Just given it a bit of thought. He is very old.

Hovstad Why the hell did you apply for that clerk's job? You haven't got a chance in hell.

Billing I don't want to get it. That's the point. I want them to reject my application. Give me something to kick against. Nothing ever happens here.

Hovstad (*writing*) No, it doesn't.

Billing They'll have to listen to me at some point. I'd better write that appeal to the Property Owners' Association.

Billing goes into the room on the right. Hovstad sits at his desk and chews his pen.

Hovstad God, this place. God, these people.

There is a knock at the door.

Come in.

Petra comes in from outside. Hovstad gets up.

Petra Hello.

Hovstad Hello. I wasn't expecting you.

Petra I'm sorry, I . . .

Hovstad Sit down. Please.

Hovstad pulls up an armchair for her.

Petra I can't stay.

Hovstad That's a shame. Did you come for your father? Did he forget something?

Petra No.

She takes out a book from her coat pocket.

It's the novel.

Hovstad It is.

Petra I can't translate it for you.

Hovstad I thought you wanted to.

Petra That was before I knew what it was about. You haven't read it, have you?

Hovstad I don't read a word of English. Thank God.

Petra You can't serialise this.

Hovstad Why? What's wrong with it?

Petra It's the antithesis of everything you believe in.

Hovstad And?

Petra It's about a force that takes care of the good and dispenses with the bad. It's hokum.

Hovstad The public love a bit of hokum with their morning coffee.

Petra And you would put your name to publishing such trash?

Hovstad Don't shoot the editor. They buy the paper for the flotsam on the back pages, which means they may digest the politics on the front pages. People like to read rubbish, it's reassuring.

Petra I didn't think you were such a Machiavel.

Hovstad Men don't get anywhere by being nice. You're a woman – you must know that? Actually, Billing has to take credit for the idea, not me. If there's a dark prince at work it's him, not me.

Petra Billing.

Hovstad I'd never heard of the story. He insisted we took it on.

Petra But Billing's an idealist.

Hovstad Totally. He's such an idealist that he's applied for the post of secretary to our local magistrate.

Petra He wouldn't do that.

Hovstad Ask him.

Petra He couldn't.

Hovstad (*looking at her more closely*) Why are you so surprised?

Petra No reason.

Hovstad We're a load of worthless hacks, Miss Stockmann.

Petra You don't mean that.

Hovstad Don't I?

Petra You're about to run a huge story that puts you all at risk.

Hovstad Which is today's news, yes.

Petra You're doing a great thing. Championing a man who is . . .

Hovstad Who is . . .

Petra A man with integrity. Honour.

Hovstad Who is your father.

Petra Yes.

Hovstad He's your father, Miss Petra. Your pa.

Petra I don't see the relevance.

Hovstad I do.

Petra What?

Hovstad I see the relevance. It's very pertinent to me.

Petra Are you teasing me?

Hovstad No.

Petra Mr Hovstad. What are you saying?

Hovstad I don't see what's quite so shameful about it.
To want to please you?

Petra I'll never believe a word that you say to me again.

Hovstad Why are you so angry?

Petra You said to Pa it was about the truth. The good of
the people. And now you . . . I can't . . . It's very . . .
disappointing.

Hovstad Don't look at me like I'm the Devil. Please.
Christ. If you had any sense, you'd be a bit nice to me.

Petra What?

Hovstad Your father needs my help.

Petra You're very low.

Hovstad I wasn't saying . . . No. No, I was . . . You're
reading me all wrong. All I meant was . . .

Petra Goodbye, Mr Hovstad.

Aslaksen rushes in from the printing office.

Aslaksen Mr Hovstad, Hovstad!

He sees Petra.

Oh excuse me. Bugger. Sorry.

Petra There's your book. Find someone else you want to . . . to translate it.

She walks towards the door.

Hovstad Miss Petra –

Petra Goodbye.

She leaves.

Aslaksen Mr Hovstad, please.

Hovstad What is it?

Aslaksen The Mayor's in the printing room.

Hovstad What?

Aslaksen He wants to talk to you. He came in the back way.

Hovstad Right.

Hovstad goes towards the printing room and opens the door. He bows and invites the Mayor in.

Could you make sure no one comes in please, Mr Aslaksen?

Aslaksen Yes, Mr Hovstad.

Aslaksen goes into the printing office.

Mayor You weren't expecting me.

Hovstad No. No, I wasn't.

Mayor You've done it up nicely here.

Hovstad Not really.

Mayor I'm taking up your valuable time.

Hovstad What can I do for you?

He takes the Mayor's hat and stick and puts them on a chair. The Mayor sits at the table.

Mayor Thank you.

Hovstad sits.

Something, something quite regrettable has happened today, Mr Hovstad.

Hovstad I expect you encounter regret on a daily basis.

Mayor I'm sorry?

Hovstad At the Council.

Mayor Today's problem concerns the Medical Officer at the Baths.

Hovstad Your brother?

Mayor He's written what he calls a report. He's submitted it to the Committee. Listing defects in the infrastructure of the buildings.

Hovstad No? Really? What's that all about, then?

Mayor He said he'd told you about it.

Hovstad Oh. Yes. I think he did mention it.

Aslaksen (*from the printing office*) I'll be needing that report now.

Hovstad (*irritated*) It's . . . it's on the main desk.

Aslaksen comes in and sees it on the desk.

Aslaksen Right you are.

Mayor But that's it, there!

Aslaksen This?

Hovstad Oh. Is that what you were talking about?

Hovstad Yes, sir, it's the Doctor's condemnation of the Baths, Your Worship

Mayor Yes, yes! Have you read it?

Hovstad Yes. I mean . . .

Mayor And?

Hovstad I haven't got a degree in streptococci. I just . . . skimmed it.

Mayor But you're printing it?

Hovstad We receive submissions. And we print them.

Aslaksen I've no say in what gets put in or not, Your Worship. They give me the thing. I print it.

Mayor I know that, Mr Aslaksen.

Aslaksen If you'll excuse me . . .

Aslaksen walks towards the printing office.

Mayor Just one moment, Mr Aslaksen. If I might, Mr Hovstad?

Hovstad Of course.

Mayor Mr Aslaksen, you're a man of intelligence, discrimination.

Aslaksen Thank you very much, Your Worship.

Mayor You've a lot of influence in various circles.

Aslaksen The workers show me a lot of respect, sir.

Mayor Those workers are the majority here. You know their opinion, I suspect, on most matters?

Aslaksen I'd say so, Your Worship.

Mayor And they'd be in favour of these repairs?

Aslaksen I'd reckon so, Your Worship. Yes. One hundred per cent.

Mayor Good. If they're determined to raise this vast amount, those who have so little . . .

Aslaksen I'm sorry?

Hovstad Who's raising what?

Mayor It's to be commended. It demonstrates a very fine public spirit. I hadn't expected they'd be prepared to look to their own pockets.

Aslaksen I'm not quite with you, Your Worship.

Mayor The ratepayers are going to have to dig hard to find it.

Hovstad Which ratepayers?

Aslaksen It's surely the shareholders who'll be footing . . .

Mayor We're talking about upwards of three hundred thousand crowns here.

Aslaksen Which is a lot of money. However . . .

Mayor Our only option is to raise it through a municipal loan.

Hovstad (*getting up*) You can't be saying it's down to the man on the street . . .?

Aslaksen You'd raise the rates to find it? Tax the working man?

Mayor Where else is the money to come from, Mr Aslaksen?

Aslaksen From those who own the Baths, I would have thought!

Mayor The Committee can't authorise any further expenditure. If the people want change, the people will have to foot the bill.

Aslaksen I . . . Mr Hovstad, this was not my understanding of the situation.

Hovstad Nor mine.

Mayor The Baths will have to shut up shop, of course. A year or two. Maybe three.

Aslaksen We wouldn't survive a total shutdown. What revenue are we going to live on?

Mayor It's a conundrum, Mr Aslaksen. But what choice is left us? We won't get a single visitor. No one will set foot in this town if they hear my brother's theory that it's rife with infection, will they?

Aslaksen It's not just a theory though, is it?

Mayor At present there's nothing conclusive. It's still speculative.

Aslaksen That's just madness. I thought . . . That's morally reprehensible of the Doctor to . . . I'm sorry, Your Worship, I was forgetting . . .

Mayor I don't relish hearing my brother talked about in those terms, but I have to concede that you're right. He was always impulsive.

Aslaksen And you're still behind him on this, Mr Hovstad?

Hovstad I don't know where I am.

Mayor I have written a brief document about how the Baths could be improved, gradually and within the means of the Committee's funds.

Hovstad Do you have it with you?

The Mayor feels in his pocket.

Mayor Do I? Oh yes. I seem to have it here.

Aslaksen He's here, look.

Mayor My brother?

Hovstad Where?

Aslaksen He's walking through the print room.

Mayor I'd rather not see him.

Hovstad points towards the door on the right.

Hovstad Go in there with Billing until he's gone.

Aslaksen Quickly, Your Worship. He's coming in.

Mayor Try to get rid of him quickly, would you?

Aslaksen ushers the Mayor through the door on the right, then closes it behind him.

Hovstad Look like you're doing something.

Hovstad sits and writes. Aslaksen looks through a pile of newspapers on a chair. Stockmann enters from the printing office. He puts down his hat and stick.

Stockmann Hello. I'm back.

Hovstad That was quick. Have you finished checking that? We're very behind schedule, aren't we?

Aslaksen Yes.

Stockmann I don't suppose there are any proofs for me to have a look through yet?

Aslaksen (*without turning to him*) We're not superhuman, Doctor.

Stockmann No. Course not. I'm just anxious . . . I can't rest till I see that article ready for printing.

Hovstad It won't be set for hours yet, will it?

Aslaksen Hours.

Stockmann Oh. I'll come back, then. Thanks.

He starts to go, but returns.

There's something else I need to talk to you about.

Hovstad This isn't a good time, actually.

Stockmann It's only two words.

Hovstad Yes.

Stockmann Torchlight procession.

Hovstad What?

Stockmann Just when the public read it. If they feel inclined to make a fuss of me. I just don't want them to. Make a fuss.

Hovstad Look, Doctor . . . I can't lie to you . . .

Stockmann What? Someone's approached you already? I'm trusting you and Aslaksen to nip it in the bud.

Hovstad Doctor, we may as well tell you now . . .

Mrs Stockmann, in a hat and cloak, enters from outside.

Mrs Stockmann Thomas.

Hovstad Mrs Stockmann. Well, we're all here.

Stockmann What on earth are you doing here, Catherine?

Mrs Stockmann Why do you think I'm here?

Hovstad Won't you sit down?

Catherine No. Thank you. I have come to collect my husband. The father of my three children.

Stockmann What?

Catherine You have three dependants and myself.

Stockmann I am acutely aware of my duties as a father and husband. I am also bound to fulfil my purpose as a human being.

Catherine You never recognised the notion of restraint, did you?

Aslaksen Restraint! That's it. That's my word exactly.

Catherine And as for you, Mr Hovstad, I don't appreciate your using my husband as a pawn in your game against the authorities.

Stockmann I'm not a pawn, for God's sake! If you must make an analogy, I'm nearer to a king, thank you.

Mrs Stockmann You're such an innocent. You realise he'll lose his position if you print this report of his?

Hovstad I didn't know that, no.

Stockmann Threats! Sticks and stones! They won't dare, Catherine. I'll have the majority behind me.

Mrs Stockmann You think that will honestly help?

Stockmann Go home now, Catherine. You take care of the house and I'll take care of society. Why are you so frightened? Truth will always out. Every liberal-minded citizen in this town will walk with me. (*He stops by a chair.*) What's this?

Aslaksen (*to himself*) Bugger.

Stockmann The crown of authority.

He picks up the Mayor's hat and holds it in the air.

He's been here. To try and talk you out of it. And then he saw me. And ran away? (*He laughs.*) Did he scarper, Mr Aslaksen?

Aslaksen Scarpered. Yes.

Stockmann He spontaneously combusted and all that was left of him was his hat and his stick. No. He never leaves them anywhere. Where is he? Where have you hidden him? Catherine, you must stay for this.

Mrs Stockmann Thomas, please. Don't.

Stockmann puts on the mayoral hat and takes his stick. He throws open the door on the right and salutes. The Mayor comes in, fuming. Billing follows him.

Mayor What is the meaning of this circus?

Stockmann A touch more respect, Peter. I am the mayor now!

He walks up and down. Mrs Stockmann fights back her tears.

Mrs Stockmann Take it off, Thomas. Please.

Mayor Give me my hat and stick now!

Stockmann You be the chief of police, I'll be the mayor.

Mayor That hat is an official emblem.

Stockmann It's a bloody hat! You threaten to sack me! I'm going to bloody sack you, Peter! I'm going to bloody sack you! Me and the rest of this town. Hovstad, the *Messenger*, Aslaksen.

Aslaksen No I won't, Doctor.

Stockmann Yes you bloody will!

Mayor You still have Hovstad.

Hovstad No. Not me.

Aslaksen Hovstad's not going to let his whole paper go down the pan just because you've been hearing voices.

Stockmann What?

Hovstad You veiled the truth, Doctor, and therefore I withdraw my support.

Billing His Worship told me everything in there. It's a scandal!

Stockmann Every word in my report is the truth. You just bloody print it. I'll deal with any hecklers.

Hovstad I'm not printing it. I can't print it.

Stockmann You're the editor. What you say goes.

Aslaksen A paper survives by dint of its readership. If your article goes out tomorrow, the whole community will suffer a recession.

Stockmann I see.

Mayor Hat. Stick. Give it me.

Stockmann takes off the hat and puts it on the table together with the stick. The Mayor takes them.

Your reign was a short one.

Stockmann I'm not dead yet. You refuse to print it, then?

Hovstad I do. For the sake of your family besides anything else.

Mrs Stockmann You leave my family out of this, Mr Hovstad!

The Mayor takes a paper from his pocket.

Mayor This will tell the public everything they need to know. It's an official statement. Mr Hovstad?

Hovstad takes the paper.

Hovstad I'll get someone to set it up. Now.

Stockmann And not mine? You think you can silence me? Mr Aslaksen, I'd like four hundred, no make that six

69

hundred copies of my pamphlet. What do you want, a cheque or cash?

Aslaksen I wouldn't do it for gold. You won't find a printer anywhere in town who'll do that job for you. They daren't.

Stockmann Give that to me.

Hovstad gives him the manuscript. Stockmann takes his own hat and stick.

It's not difficult to disclose information. I'll hold a public meeting.

Mayor No one will rent you a hall.

Aslaksen They won't.

Mrs Stockmann Why have they all turned against you, Tom?

Stockmann Because the men in this town are in fact little old women. All they can think about is their little lives. There's nothing beyond that.

Mrs Stockmann Then I'll be a man with you, Tom. All the way.

Stockmann Thank you. Thank you, my love. The truth will be told. If I can't hire a hall, I'll get Eilif to play his drum and I'll shout it out from every street corner.

Mayor They'll think you're a lunatic.

Stockmann I'd rather be labelled a lunatic than a liar and a coward.

Aslaksen You'll be alone.

Mrs Stockmann No, he won't. Our boys will be beside him.

Stockmann And Petra! And you!

Mrs Stockmann Tom, I can't. I just can't. But I'll watch you. And bless you.

He puts his arm around her.

Stockmann You go and make your big noise, gentlemen. We'll see whether mediocrity can win over genius.

The Stockmanns leave together.

Mayor Mad. He's quite mad. And he's driven her insane as well.

Act Four

*A large, old-fashioned hall in Captain Horster's house.
At the back open double-leaved doors lead to a lobby.
There are three windows in the left hand wall. There is
a dais on which stands a small table set with two candles,
a carafe of water, a glass and a bell. This might be set so
that it faces the audience as if they were the crowd from
the town. Bracket lamps give more light between the
windows. On the left is a table with a candle and a chair
next to it. On the right is a door with a few chairs near it.
There are a few Townspeople in the room.*

Man 1 (*to Lamstad*) Lamstad. The world and his bloody
wife turning up, eh?

Man 2 You have to keep up with what's going on.

Man 3 What is going on?

Man 1 He's got his whistle!

Man 3 Aye! Evensen's brung his horn and all!

Man 1 Dr Stockmann's going to attack the Mayor.

Man 2 That's his brother, in't it?

Man 3 Makes no odds to Dr Stockmann.

Man 2 He's wrong though, in't he? Paper said.

Man 1 Nobody let him have a hall because he's wrong.
Not the Baths, nor the POA.

Man 2 Whose side are we on, then?

Man 3 Don't ask me. Likely we go the same road as
Aslaksen, eh?

Billing passes by with a briefcase.

Billing Excuse me. I'm reporting for the paper. Thank you.

He sits down at the table on the left. Captain Horster escorts Mrs Stockmann and Petra in from the right-hand door.

Horster If you'd like to sit here? So if you need to leave at any point . . .

Mrs Stockmann Why should we need to leave?

Horster No reason.

Mrs Stockmann and Petra sit down.

Mrs Stockmann It was very kind of you to offer my husband this room.

Petra It was very brave, Captain Horster.

Horster Not at all.

Hovstad and Aslaksen come through the crowd separately.

Aslaksen Shouldn't the Doctor be here by now?

Horster He's in the other room. Waiting.

The Mayor enters. The Towns people acknowledge him

Hovstad Here's the Mayor.

Billing Well. This is going to be interesting.

The Mayor gently makes his way through while greeting folk, and stands against the wall on the left. Stockmann enters through the right-hand door. He wears black, a frock coat, a white cravat. There are a few uncertain claps swiftly followed by hisses. Silence.

Stockmann Cathy? Are you all right?

Mrs Stockmann I'm fine. Just don't let them rile you, Tom.

Stockmann I'll be as calm as the sea.

He looks at his watch, steps up on to the dais and bows. He takes out his manuscript.

It's quarter past now. Let's . . . We'll . . . make a start, shall we?

Aslaksen Who's the chairman?

Stockmann Chairman? We don't need one.

Man 1/2/3 (*simultaneously*) Who says we don't need a chairman? / We've got to have a chairman. / Who says we don't need 'im?

Mayor I think it would be an idea to have someone in the chair.

Stockmann Peter, all I'm doing is giving a speech?

Mayor The Doctor's speech may give rise to argument, *ergo* we need a Chair.

Man 1/2/3 Chair! / Chair! / Chair! / Chair!

Hovstad You'd better have one.

Stockmann Very well. So?

Aslaksen Perhaps the Mayor would do us the honour. Your Worship?

Man 1/2/3 Hear hear! / Hear hear!

Mayor Thank you. But I must decline the honour for personal reasons. I nominate Mr Aslaksen, Chairman of the Property Owners' Association.

Voices Hurrah! Get Aslaksen up there!

Aslaksen steps up on to the dais. Stockmann steps down.

Billing Go on, Aslaksen!

Aslaksen You know my philosophy, gentlemen. Restraint. I'm a peace-loving man. Moderation is a wonderful thing.

Drunk Three cheers for the Temperance Society!

Aslaksen Sobriety too, in mind and body.

Drunk Sober! Sober! Hip-hip-hooray, hip-hip-hip . . .

Man 1 Oi! Shut it!

Voices Shh.

Aslaksen I would request that our fellow citizen who has called this meeting conducts himself fittingly and stays within the limits of moderation.

Drunk Hear hear!

Aslaksen Interruption is not debate, sir. Does anyone have anything constructive to say before we commence? The floor is open.

Mayor Mr Chairman!

Aslaksen Your Worship!

Mayor I find myself in a delicate position. Dr Stockmann is . . . You all know we are brothers. I'd therefore prefer to keep . . . mum! But my official capacity compels me to speak. I propose that no one here would wish to witness libel against our Baths. Our livelihood. Am I right?

Voices You're right there, Your Worship! Hear hear! Yes!

Mayor I therefore move that this meeting should not be allowed to take place.

Stockmann What? What are you saying?

Mrs Stockmann coughs.

You're refusing my right to the freedom of speech?

Mayor If I may continue?

Stockmann Go on.

Mayor Everyone knows the facts. I laid them out for all to read in *The People's Messenger.* I pointed out the fallacy that the Baths are contaminated. I also outlined the amount required, gentlemen, should drastic measures be taken. Just to make a start on the work we'd need upwards of a hundred thousand crowns. Which would mean an immediate and significant rise in your present income tax.

Whistles and grunts.
Aslaksen rings his bell.

Aslaksen *Silentium*, gentlemen! Order! If I might add something. Firstly, I'm all for self-government, but not when implementing it means the financial crippling of the working man. Secondly, that I do believe the Doctor to be honest. But misguided. And, and it pains me to say this, he is not without revolutionary leanings. Therefore I second the Mayor's motion to put an end to this meeting.

Assent from the crowd.

Hovstad I'd like to add something, Mr Chairman. The fact is Dr Stockmann misled us. He distorted the facts.

Stockmann I did not!

Hovstad He coloured them, then. I'm all for freedom of expression. *The People's Messenger* under my leadership is a champion of it. But when it comes to vital issues like this, and misrepresentation, we must proceed with caution.

Aslaksen Restraint. Yes.

Hovstad I ask you, my friends. Is it not the duty of an editor to promote the welfare of his readers, of the people? Tell me if I'm wrong. I'm prepared to be wrong.

Voices No! / No, you're right! / Hovstad's on the money there!

Hovstad The Doctor has always been well-liked. I have enjoyed his generous hospitality on many an occasion. But he has lost any sense of perspective over this issue. His findings are grossly exaggerated. The Baths are now wary of keeping him on in his present capacity. And yet, despite the threat of dismissal, with the possibility of destitution just around the corner, not just for himself but for his wife and three children, the Doctor still continues with this tirade.

Stockmann You leave my family out of this, Hovstad!

Hovstad A man who abandons his family –

Petra Keep to the business in hand, sir!

Mrs Stockmann Petra. Please.

Aslaksen I shall now put the Mayor's resolution to the vote.

Stockmann Don't. There's no need. I've nothing to say to you about the Baths. I wish to talk to you about something quite different.

Mayor What?

Drunk I pay my taxes. My bloody bloody bloody bloody bleeding taxes. So I've a right to speak. I do. So I do.

Voices Shut up! / Be quiet. / Chuck him out. / Bloody drunks.

The drunk is ejected from the room.

Stockmann May I speak now?

Aslaksen rings the bell. Morten Kiil watches Stockmann.

Aslaksen The floor is yours.

Stockmann My friends. The last few days have been almost like a fever for me. I'm going to share something with you which is far more important than the fact that the Baths are poisoned. That fact is no longer so relevant.

Voices Oi! Oi! He said he weren't going to mention that! / Not the Baths they said! / No Baths! / They're bloody relevant to me! / And me!

Stockmann What I've realised is that our spiritual lives are tainted. Our community is based upon lie after bloody lie.

Voices What's he saying? / Eh? / I'm no liar. / Language!

Mayor That's just ridiculous.

Aslaksen I must request the speaker to moderate his language and exercise restraint.

Stockmann I was born here. I love these streets. These forests. Moving away to a medical practice in a backwater was very hard. Harsh. There was such poverty up north that I sometimes thought a vet would be more useful to the community than a doctor. I ached to be back here. It's the most beautiful place that I know.

A few claps.

I had just one desire when I returned. To work for the absolute good of the people.

Mayor So when did that change?

Stockmann I was so happy to be living here again that . . . that I was almost blinded with my love of this town. The night before last my eyes opened for the first time. I saw the hypocrisy of the authorities. Their imbecility.

Mayor Mr Chairman!

Aslaksen rings his bell.

Aslaksen By the authority vested in me, Dr Stockmann!

Stockmann Authority, yes! I saw the absolute stupidity of those in power. These pseudo-politicians. They have such a primal need to invade or destroy. I'd like to see them shot at dawn.

Unrest.

Mayor Are we supposed to listen to this?

Aslaksen rings his bell.

Aslaksen Dr Stockmann, that's enough!

Stockmann My brother has always loved power. Since he could first grab something out of one's hand. You like to control, don't you, Peter?

Laughter, confusion. The Drunk has reappeared.

Drunk I knew a woman! She loved to control! Always always on top, she was.

Man 1 Who is he? He's not from round here.

Aslaksen Get that man out! He's not even a local drunk!

The Drunk is thrown out again.

Stockmann It's not the politicians, though, who are the real danger. No, they're old. They're already on their way out. Their thoughts will be buried with them very soon. They don't need any reminders from me of their mortality. No. They are not the deadliest enemies of freedom and truth.

Voices Who is then? / Who's the enemy?/ Who is it?

Stockmann I was coming to that. The most dangerous public enemy is the majority! The liberal-minded bloody majority! You! All of you!

Complete uproar. Stamping, shouting, whistling.
Chaos reigns for a few moments but Aslaksen keeps
ringing his bell until silence prevails.

Aslaksen I move that the speaker retract those heinous remarks.

Stockmann Why? You're all tightening the gag over my mouth. Who forms the majority? The wise or the foolish? You have to concede that idiots outnumber geniuses. Are you telling me the average man should rule over the great?

Shouts and stamping.

Shout, that's it! Shout! It doesn't make you right. The minority will always be the pioneers for justice!

Hovstad You've joined their ranks, have you? Of this intellectual aristocracy? Over the last two days?

Stockmann Possibly! Yes, there are only a few amongst us who discover new truths! I'm tired of the mundane. The mediocre. Those who seek the truth, they have to wait for the herd to catch up.

Hovstad You've become a revolutionary as well, have you?

Stockmann Yes, I have! I want to start a revolution against the bare-faced lie that truth is monopolised by the majority. Truth shifts. You don't seem to realise that over the centuries what were truths reconfigure as lies. Do you know what the average age of a truth is? Eighteen years. The older a truth becomes, the thinner it gets. Majority truths are like rotting meat. They are the cause of the moral scurvy that our community is in the grip of.

Aslaksen It seems to me that the honoured speaker has strayed from the text.

Mayor I second that. What the hell is he talking about? He's gone off on a complete tangent.

Stockmann Oh Peter, my brother, I really do think you've lost your mind. Every point I'm making is deeply relevant. My point is this. The majority encourage stagnation, ignorance, they balk against anything that's other, that's more elevated than the average worker's house. What we hold as indisputable truths were unveiled by progressive thinkers in our grandparents' time. We can't stick to those archaic notions. There is only one real truth. That no society can grow if it feeds on beliefs that were in vogue in biblical times.

Hovstad Such as?

Voice Yes! / Example! / Give us an example, if you're so bloody clever!

Stockmann There's hundreds out there. All right. Take the supposed truth that the common man has as much right to sanction and condemn, to advise and to govern as those few who are intellectually superior.

Billing This is really not good.

Hovstad Listen to this, my friends! He's taking away your human rights!

Voices So we're no good, are we? / Is that what he's saying? / Chuck him out! / Blow your horn, Evensen!

Evensen blows his horn. General commotion.

Stockmann Hovstad, don't look at me like I was the devil. I thought you above all would be with me on this one. You're a freethinker.

Voices Hovstad, is it? / A freethinker?

Hovstad Prove it! Show me that in writing.

Stockmann I see. Of course, of course you never put it in writing. You're a closet freethinker. Well, I'll be the only outed freethinker, then. I don't see why you're all so outraged about the notion of difference. If you look at the animal kingdom everything has a hierarchy and every animal has a different ability. An old dog on the street can't run like a greyhound. A stunted chicken hasn't the qualities of a Japanese hen.

Voices What's he on about? / I'm not a dog.

Hovstad We're not animals sir!

Stockmann But we are, sir, that's exactly what we are! That's as much as we can hope for. And we have our own pecking order, just as they have. Don't you see, as long as you're trying to keep the majority happy you'll never aspire to anything higher than a mindless mongrel, Hovstad? Anything nobler?

Hovstad I'm working-class and proud, Stockmann. Proud!

Stockmann It's not a question of class. Look at my brother. Apparently he's very high up on the social ladder. No. All he's ever doing is just stretching up to earwig the talk and thoughts of those a few rungs higher than him. And then he emulates them. He's the head of the mob. We're actually descended from pirates, aren't we, Peter?

Mayor Just shut up, Thomas!

Stockmann My brother is a gangster and thug *par excellence*.

Mayor I object. I object!

Stockmann He's a slave to the mob's mentality and can't sleep at night for fear of the liberals.

Mayor Mr Chairman!

Hovstad Are you saying you've got to be descended from royalty to be progressive?

Stockmann I'm saying that, yes, being distinguished in some sense is nothing to be ashamed of! Your liberalism at the *People's Messenger*, Hovstad, your so-called liberalism is actually veiled morality. You're inclined to preach the idea that culture demoralises society! Well, that's a fetid lie. It's stupidity, ignorance and foul living conditions that turn us into brutes. If you live in filth how can you hope to think about anything on a higher plane than the grease-spotted window you stare out of? You all want to build this town up? On the basis of a foul stinking cesspit?

Aslaksen You can't say that!

Voices Make him stand down. / Yes, yes! / Down, down, down!

Stockmann I'll stand down! Don't you tell me what to do! I'll stand down when I want to. And now I want to. But I'm not going away. I am going to publicise this situation from the outside! I'll write to every publication and rag in the country!

Hovstad You really are hell bent on our destruction, aren't you?

Stockmann I love this town intensely. I'm wedded to it. Nobody wants to see their bride become syphilitic.

Aslaksen Retract that, sir. Retract that!

Shouts.

Hovstad This man wants to kill off our livelihoods. He is an enemy of the people.

Stockmann A town that lives a lie ought to die. You'll infect the whole country. You should be shot, the lot of you!

Voice He's an enemy of the people! / He been drinking!

Billing You heard it here! An enemy of the people! The voice of the people!

Voices He's a bloody alcoholic! / Bloody lunatic!

Billing Enemy! Enemy! Enemy of the people!

Voices Enemy! Enemy! / Enemy of the people!

Aslaksen Gentlemen! I'm shocked. Shocked by what I have heard tonight. An enemy of the people is not a phrase to be bandied about. But I'm forced to propose this motion. This meeting puts to the vote that Dr Thomas Stockmann is hereby named an enemy of the people. We need to cast a vote, but to prevent anything underhand it will be anonymous. Do you have some paper there, Mr Billing?

Billing I've white or blue.

Aslaksen Both. Give me both. I shall put the papers in my hat. Take a blue paper if you disagree with the motion. A white if you're in agreement that the Doctor is an enemy to the people. Are we clear?

Voices Aye. / Aye. / Aye.

The Drunk raises his hand.

Drunk Nay! Neigh . . . neigh . . . neigh . . . (*He giggles and makes horse like sounds.*) She used to piss like a horse against a big old tree.

The Mayor leaves. Aslaksen goes around with his hat. Morten Kiil approaches Stockmann.

Morten You see what your monkey tricks have led to?

Stockmann I have done my duty.

Morten And you stand by the fact that the tanneries are the root of the pollution?

Stockmann I do.

Morten Mine included?

Stockmann Yours is the worst offender. What do you want, Morten Kiil?

Morten You'd put that in the paper? About my tannery? My father's tannery?

Stockmann Yes. Yes I would.

Morten Kiil exits.

Drunk I want a white paper. And a blue paper. And a white paper. No. Blue. Blue.

The Drunk takes a blue paper. All the others who Aslaksen has approached have taken a white paper. A businessman, Vik, approaches Captain Horster.

Vik I'm surprised at you, Horster.

Horster I think I can do with my property what I please, Mr Vik.

Vik I'll be in touch tomorrow.

Vik Exits.

Petra Who was that, Captain Horster?

Horster Edvard Vik. He owns the Kristiana Line.

Aslaksen This gathering of citizens declares almost unanimously, in fact unanimously as the exception was inebriated and foreign, that Dr Stockmann is considered an enemy of the people. Long live our Mayor! Long live our brilliant Mayor, who has so loyally suppressed the voice of blood!

Cheers.

The meeting is closed.

Billing Well done, Aslaksen. Well done!

Stockmann Petra. My hat. Coat. Captain. Are there still berths on your ship? When do you sail for America?

Horster There's always room for you and yours, Doctor.

Stockmann Good. Catherine. Petra.

Mrs Stockmann We can go out this way.

Stockmann takes her arm.

Stockmann No. We walk out the way we came in. You'll hear more of this! I'm not as forgiving as the Almighty. I've turned my cheek so many times it's worn to the bone.

Aslaksen That's blasphemy, Doctor!

Voices He's threatening us now. / Break his windows! / Throw him in the fjord! / Horn Evensen, get your horn out!

Evensen blows his horn. Commotion. Captain Horster leads them out.

Billing Damn you! Damn you, Stockmann! Damn you and your bourgeois drinking parties!

Voices can be heard outside.

Voices (*outside*) Enemy! Enemy! Enemy of the people! Enemy! Enemy! Enemy of the people!

Act Five

Stockmann's study. Morning. There are books and cupboards containing medicine bottles along the walls. On the back wall is the door to the hallway, to the left is the door to the living room. On the right-hand wall are two windows, which have been smashed. In the middle is a desk covered with books and papers. The room is in chaos.

Stockmann, in dressing gown, slippers and smoking hat, crouches down under one of the cupboards with an umbrella. He manages to hook the offending stone. He speaks into the living room.

Stockmann Catherine! I've found another.

Catherine Yes.

Stockmann (*putting the stone into a pile on the table*) I shall keep these as sacred relics. (*Shouts.*) Has . . . what's-her-name gone for the glazier yet? The maid?

Mrs Stockmann enters.

Mrs Stockmann He doesn't know if he can manage it today.

Stockmann Or any other day, I expect.

Mrs Stockmann There's a letter for you.

She gives it to him. He opens it and reads it.

Stockmann It's a notice. To vacate the premises.

Mrs Stockmann Oh.

Stockmann He's 'terribly sorry', 'regretful', etcetera, etcetera. No matter. America's the place.

87

Mrs Stockmann Is it?

Stockmann They tore my best trousers. The first lesson of freedom fighting, never wear your favourite clothes when you go to meet the mob.

Mrs Stockmann Leaving is a huge decision.

Stockmann They're probably not much better in America. The majority's rampant there too. But at least it's more dispersed. They'll kill you. But they won't torture you slowly like a cat with a bird. What I really need is a primeval forest. Or a South Sea island that's gone bust.

Mrs Stockmann The boys need friends.

Stockmann You think they'll find pals among these lunatics? These dullards?

Petra enters.

Mrs Stockmann Did you forget something?

Petra No. I've been sacked.

Stockmann Sacked?

Petra Well, Mrs Busk gave me my notice. Two weeks. So I just walked out.

Stockmann Good for you. Well done.

Petra She said she dared not do otherwise.

Stockmann Splendid. Splendid.

Petra She received three letters this morning. Anonymous. One said that I held excessively free views on a range of subjects . . .

Stockmann Pack your bags, Petra. Get ready. We're leaving as soon as Horster confirms our passage.

Mrs Stockmann Shh. There's someone just come in.

Petra opens the door to outside.

Petra It's you, Captain Horster. Come in.

Horster (*from the hall*) Good morning. I just came by to see how everything stood.

He enters.

Stockmann Thank you. That's good of you.

Mrs Stockmann Thank you for walking us home last night, Captain.

Petra Did you get back to your house without any trouble?

Horster Yes. They shouted a bit.

Stockmann They're quite incredible cowards, aren't they? Look. Most of these are pebbles, not even rocks. And they all stood out there yelling, threatening to beat me to a pulp. But no one actually stepped over the threshold. It's that phrase though – enemy of the people. It's like a needle scratching my lung. It feels caught in my throat.

Petra They're just cavemen, Father.

Horster Public opinion always shifts and changes.

Stockmann Quite. Their punishment is their existence. So when do we sail, Captain?

Horster That's why I'm here actually.

Stockmann Is there a problem?

Horster I shan't be sailing with her.

Petra They haven't taken your ship away?

Horster (*smiles*) Yes. They have.

Petra I don't believe it.

Mrs Stockmann Oh, Thomas. You see.

Stockmann My friend, if I'd known, if I'd had any idea . . .

Horster Don't worry on my account. Plenty of other ships in the sea.

Stockmann Damn. Damn. If only you hadn't seen us home perhaps this wouldn't have happened.

Horster I've no regrets.

Petra holds out her hand to him.

Petra Thank you, Captain.

Horster If you still want to make the trip there is another way.

Stockmann Can it be soon?

A knock at the door.

Mrs Stockmann Shh.

Petra I think it's Uncle.

Stockmann Is it? Ha! Come in!

The Mayor enters from the hall.

Mayor You've company. I'll come back later.

Stockmann No. Come in. Please.

Mayor I wanted a word privately.

Mrs Stockmann We'll leave you alone, then.

Horster I'll call back later.

Stockmann No. Go in with them. I want to hear about this . . .

Horster I'll wait, then.

Mrs Stockmann, Petra and Captain Horster go into the living room. The Mayor is silent. He looks at the windows.

Stockmann I'm sorry if there's a draught. Perhaps you should put your hat on.

Mayor I'm sorry. That last night became what it did.

Stockmann Is that it?

Mayor This is from the directors.

He gives him a large letter.

Stockmann My dismissal?

Mayor We had no choice.

Stockmann Nobody around here seems to have much choice lately.

Mayor You should leave town for a while.

Stockmann I may well do.

Mayor In six months' time you can retract your statement. 'I regret,' etcetera.

Stockmann And go to work back at the Baths.

Mayor Possibly.

Stockmann And what would the public have to say about that?

Mayor Public opinion is like a woman, fickle. A man with responsibilities has no right to be as reckless as you, Thomas. Also it would be good. For us. The Council. We do need you to retract it.

Stockmann I'll tell you the only true duty of a man, Peter. It is not to spread excrement all over himself. Like an animal.

Mayor Yes. Well. There's no use talking to you while you're in this mood. I do know, you know.

Stockmann Know what?

Mayor The actual reason. Your material gain. I'm not unaware of what's going on.

Stockmann Then you have the advantage on me.

Mayor I know about Morten Kiil. About his will.

Stockmann He's leaving what money he has to the home for Old Artisans. So what?

Mayor Firstly, it's a vast amount he's leaving. Secondly, a significant portion of his estate is left to your children. You and your wife could live on even the interest it gains without having to work.

Stockmann Ah. Really? I didn't know that.

Mayor It's a lot of money.

Stockmann Is it? That's good. Very good. Catherine and the children will be secure. Thank you. I'll tell her.

Mayor Not yet you won't.

Stockmann I'll tell my wife what I like when I like, Peter.

Mayor Kiil can revoke the will at any time.

Stockmann Why would he? He's in Seventh Heaven with this result. He loves the fact that the Directors have been exposed.

Mayor Yes. Which is my point.

Stockmann You've lost me again, Peter. What the hell is your point?

Mayor You sullied the reputation of the Baths simply to curry favour with the old man. You were willing to have our bastion crash so that that bitter ancient degenerate would remember you in his will.

Stockmann Peter. My brother. You would think that of me? Truly?

Mayor I have no option.

Stockmann Option? Option, Peter?

Mayor We've everything we need to look clean again. Your dismissal. And now your motive for such libel.

Stockmann You're the lowest scum I have ever known. (*Pause.*) You are my brother.

Mayor I have no brother.

He leaves.

Stockmann (*shouts*) You filthy . . . filthy bastard! Catherine! Disinfect the place! Bleach it where he stood and sat! Get that girl! The maid! To decontaminate the place after his stinking rotten filth!

Mrs Stockmann enters.

Mrs Stockmann Thomas, shush! What happened?

Petra looks in.

Petra Grandfather's here, Pa. He wants to speak to you.

Stockmann Tell him to come in. Come in, come in!

Mrs Stockmann exits. Morten Kiil comes in. Stockmann closes the door after him.

Morten.

Morten I like what you've done with the place.

Stockmann Fantastic, isn't it?

Morten Lots of fresh air. You feel good after last night?

Stockmann Yes.

Morten I thought you would. I've something to show you.

He takes out a thick wallet with a wad of papers in it.

Stockmann Shares. In the Baths?

Morten They were incredibly cheap.

Stockmann Morten, these have got today's date on them.

Morten I've cashed in everything.

Stockmann But these will crash. They'll be worthless in a matter of days.

Morten Not if you act sensibly they won't.

Stockmann Everyone seems to want me to act in a particular way. What is this about, Kiil? Why the sudden need for shares in a defunct concern?

Morten You told everyone that the worst of the filth comes from my tannery.

Stockmann Because it does.

Morten My father put that place on the map. He ran it before me and his father before him. I won't have us remembered like this. Like three angels of death.

Stockmann I can't change the facts.

Morten Yes, you can. Anyone can change facts. The money I've invested. It was to go to Catherine and the children.

Stockmann You've spent their legacy.

Morten I have.

Stockmann You spent it. Their . . . You've spent it.

Morten I did. So that every time you say the tannery is infected you're hammering a nail into their little coffins.

Every time you cite it as the root of the problem you're taking food away from the mouths of your own children. Only a lunatic would do that.

Stockmann But I am a lunatic. Haven't you heard? Don't you read the local papers?

Morten Not when your wife and children are at stake.

Stockmann Why didn't you speak to me? Why? Before you bought all this . . . tissue paper?

Morten I needed to provoke you into action. It's your choice. Penury or comfort.

Stockmann I don't know why this has all spiralled into insanity. The only thing we need is a cure for the waters.

Morten Why not try rat poison? They smashed your windows then.

Stockmann I must talk to Catherine.

Morten Do. She'll know what's best.

Stockmann Why did you do this thing? Why? Why would you want to put me in such a position?

Morten Let me know by two o'clock. If you don't want to recant I'll leave the money to the Old Artisans and I'll do it today.

Stockmann And Catherine?

Morten What about her?

The door to the hall is opened. Hovstad and Aslaksen are there.

The liberals, is it?

Stockmann You are not welcome here, sirs. This is not an at-home day. And I'd like you to leave.

Hovstad We can't.

Aslaksen We need to talk to you.

Morten Two o'clock.

Morten Kiil leaves.

Stockmann What do you want? As you can see, I'm rather busy.

Hovstad We couldn't do other than we did last night.

Stockmann Damn you. Both of you.

Aslaksen Why didn't you tell us?

Stockmann Tell you what?

Aslaksen The money. Your father-in-law. The shares.

Stockmann He bought a lot of shares today, yes.

Aslaksen It's a bit obvious. Would have been a bit more sensible to get someone outside the family.

Hovstad You could have done it all anonymously. I could have helped you, Dr Stockmann.

Stockmann Helped. You could have? Helped.

Aslaksen You brought in a great axe. All you needed for the job was a paper knife.

Hovstad And it's only fair to share such a brilliant scheme.

Stockmann What do you want of me?

Hovstad We could help. The *Messenger* could smooth things out a bit.

Stockmann And in exchange?

Hovstad The real problem the paper faces is capital, you see. Money. Filthy stuff. We always wanted to help you. Give you support.

Stockmann Wonderful. That's beautiful. But aren't you forgetting a tiny detail? Who I am? I am an enemy of the people! I am a traitor to all that's decent! Where the hell is my stick?

Hovstad What? Look, if you don't want to come in with us on this we can easily make things look a lot worse for you. We'll put the shares story on the front page.

Stockmann That's right. Kick a dog while it's down!

Hovstad It's the law of nature. The fittest survive.

Aslaksen If you're not born with a silver spoon in your mouth you've got to get out there and bloody find one!

Stockmann Or steal it! Let's see who's the fittest then, shall we?

He finds his umbrella and starts to swing it.

Aslaksen Attempted assault, this is!

Stockmann Get out! Jump through the window! Climb through the broken glass, you bastard!

Hovstad You're insane! Doctor! Dr Stockmann!

Stockmann Jump! Now! Jump!

Aslaksen Restraint! Shit!

Mrs Stockmann, Petra and Captain Horster come in.

Mrs Stockmann Thomas!

Stockmann You'll bloody jump when I tell you to! Through the glass and into the gutter!

Hovstad It's attempted assault, Captain! You're my witness! Lunatic!

Hovstad walks out through the hall.

Aslaksen Bloody hell.

Aslaksen runs after him. Stockmann is hysterical.

Mrs Stockmann Tom! Tom!

She slaps his face. He goes to slap her back. Stops himself. He comes out of the hysteria slowly.

Stockmann Have they gone?

Mrs Stockmann They've gone. Tom. Tom?

Stockmann I must . . . (*He writes on a card.*) Look, Catherine.

She reads the card, he reads it with her.

'No. No. No.' Cathy. I'm sorry.

Mrs Stockmann What? What does it mean?

Stockmann Forgive me. I'll explain it later. Petra, take this to . . . to . . . to the maid. Have her deliver it to Morten Kiil now. Now.

Petra takes the card and hurries out.

Stockmann I've so much to do, Catherine. I've so much to do.

Mrs Stockmann But Tom, we're leaving. We've got to go. Now.

Petra enters.

Petra She's taken it.

Stockmann Leaving? No. No we're not. We're going to stay here. Stay and fight it out.

Petra Are we staying, Pa?

Stockmann Yes. This is our town. We'll find another house. As long as there's a roof over our head.

Horster You must stay at mine. It's a barn of a place. And I'm never there. I shan't be in your way.

Mrs Stockmann Captain Horster. You are always so kind.

Petra You are. Thank you, Captain.

Stockmann Thank you, sir. Thank you. I've all the time in the world now for this battle. I've no job. Apart from the handful of patients they won't be able to hound away from me. And I will simply keep shouting. Telling the town what's going on.

Mrs Stockmann But that's what you did last night. And they almost killed you.

Stockmann No no. Not a scratch. No. I just need to tell them that the liberals are the most insidious enemies to freedom. That shouldn't be too complicated for them to grasp, eh, Captain?

Horster Politics, Doctor, it all goes straight over my head.

Stockmann It's very simple. The party bosses are the wolves. Hungry wolves. They need to eat a good few sacrificial lambs with every new year. Aslaksen, Hovstad, they've devoured idealists who've come to them hungry for change. They eat them up, then they spit them out and they're fit for nothing. Cathy, look. At that sunlight that's coming in. The air smells good, no?

Mrs Stockmann It does.

Stockmann Don't worry, my angel. I've not lost my mind. And we'll get by. We won't be rich but we'll never starve. The only thing I worry about is the future. And who will continue to speak the truth.

Petra The boys will learn from you, Pa. And their boys will learn from them.

Stockmann The boys, yes. I'll talk to them when they get back from school.

Mrs Stockmann They're upstairs. I didn't want to tell you while your brother was here. Eilif has a split lip and Morten a black eye.

Stockmann What? How?

Mrs Stockmann They were in a fight. With the other schoolboys.

Stockmann My boys. Children. Bloodied. Blooded. At school.

Mrs Stockmann They're all right. They're fine. Dying to show you their war wounds. I think they're rather proud. Their first fight.

Stockmann It's everywhere, isn't it? It's endemic. Cruelty. Even in children. I won't have them bullied. I won't. If needs be I'll teach them at home.

Petra I'll help you, Pa. We can teach them together.

Stockmann That's it. We'll teach them. But not just them, Petra. Do you know any tykes? Who want to learn? Who have spirit? Some urchins who've got a good set of lungs on them?

Petra They're everywhere.

Stockmann We'll make Captain Horster's dining room into the School of Athens. I'll teach them to hunt all the grey wolves and chase them to the far west.

Mrs Stockmann Perhaps the grey wolves will hunt you, Tom.

Stockmann No. Me? You seem to forget, Catherine, I'm the strongest man.

Mrs Stockmann Are you?

Stockmann I learnt something. Something.

Mrs Stockmann Did you? What did you learn, Tom?

Stockmann What? Oh. Yes. Alone. The strongest man. He's always alone.

Mrs Stockmann Thomas?

Petra Pa?

Stockmann Yes. Yes. He's alone.

Lights down.